To Stephen – your patience and compassion is steadfast.

Keeping *it* OFF

MICHELLE
BRIDGES

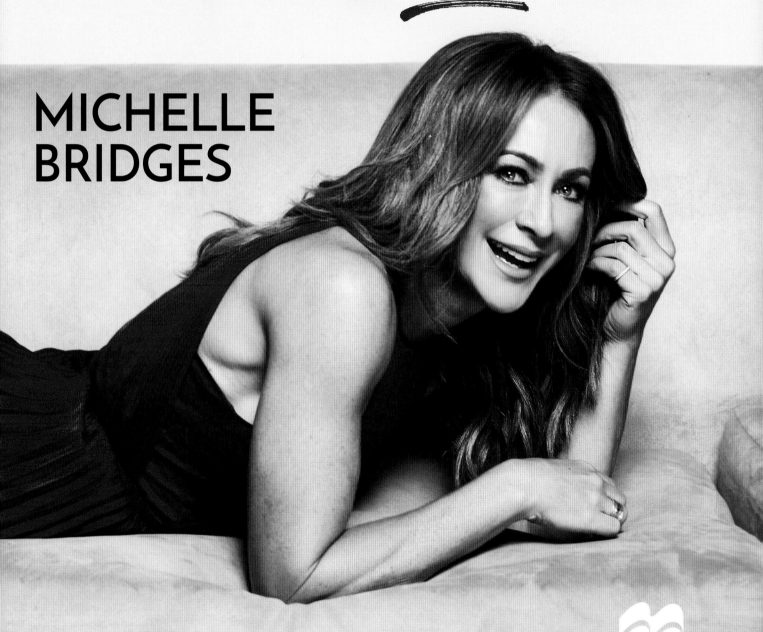

MACMILLAN
Pan Macmillan Australia

INTRODUCTION

It's time for us to have the conversation that no one else seems to be having.

This book is not about short-term weight loss, it's about the long haul. And I'm going to be honest with you: there is no magic bullet when it comes to maintaining weight loss over the long term. Sure, we can all lose weight by tidying up our diets and ramping up our exercise, but the uncomfortable truth is that, for most of us, the weight eventually creeps back on. Why? This question has been nagging me for years. In this book, I explore the factors contributing to weight regain and the habits that will give us the greatest chance of keeping weight off. And I'll be straight with you: these habits must be lifelong – you need to dig deep and stay committed.

Every few years, the Australian Bureau of Statistics conducts a National Health Survey of chronic disease risk factors. In the most recent survey (2015), an estimated 28 per cent of Australians had a body mass index (BMI) over 30, putting them in the obese category and therefore at serious risk of developing diabetes, cardiovascular disease, non-alcoholic fatty liver disease and kidney disease. That's almost one in three. And those figures don't even include people who are just overweight.

For the past thirty years, I've been helping people improve their health, fitness and headspace. And I love what I do. I love seeing their smiles when they reach a goal and hearing them talk excitedly about the positive changes they've made. It's magical watching people fire up and take charge of their lives. But here's the thing: fifteen years ago only 20 per cent of us were obese. This blew me away. How can we be getting fatter despite all the positive public education out there? What are we doing wrong?

THE STATS SAY IT ALL

Ten years ago, when I wrote my first book, *Crunch Time*, I was convinced that losing weight was pretty much a matter of eating less and moving more, and that everyone and their grandma could do it with the right mindset. Like the majority of my mates in the health and fitness industry, I saw weight management as a 'calories in–calories out' proposition: eat more than you burn and you gain weight; burn more than you eat and you lose weight. And yes, I was aware that certain nutritional, genetic, neuro-hormonal and other factors had roles to play but, for the most part, restricting calories and doing more exercise was the way to go.

Since then I've worked directly (through *The Biggest Loser*) and indirectly (through my 12 Week Body Transformation program, 12WBT) with hundreds of thousands of people to help them transform their health and fitness. Some wanted to lose *a lot* of weight (more than 30 per cent of their baseline weight) and others just a little (less than 5 per cent), and when they did they experienced *amazing* changes to their self-image, confidence, physical wellbeing, mindset and overall zest for life. The

It's time for us to have the conversation that no one else seems to be having.

7

extraordinary success of 12WBT has been based on a simple yet effective framework. Everything I talk about in this book – habits and routines for life – is an integral part of its philosophy.

However, I'm going to be straight with you: for most people, keeping the weight off is *really* hard; some say even harder than losing the weight in the first place. Indeed, long-term studies are showing that **within two years, more than 80 per cent of people who lose weight will have regained some, if not all, of it.** (And when people do wacky crash diets, without proper nutrition or exercise, 98 per cent of them will not only regain the weight, but also put on more.)

What is going on here, people? I know most of us are quick to blame ourselves for not having the willpower to stick to a healthy eating plan or to continue with our training, and that might be partly true, but seriously – *four* out of *five*? I had to dig deeper to figure out how we got ourselves into this mess. So, I reached out to my fitness and weight-loss community to see if I could unearth any trends. I asked people about their experiences of managing weight loss in the long term, and have featured some of those stories here as case studies. They were amazingly honest and generous, whether they were able to keep the weight off or not. I also did some serious research about the factors that drive weight regain and what we can do about them.

WE ARE ALL DIFFERENT

It's important to understand that you and I can eat exactly the same meals, but our bodies will metabolise the energy and nutrients very differently depending on our age, our genetic makeup, how well our thyroid functions, our lean muscle mass, how stressed we are and even how often we've dieted in the past. You see, when we diet, our bodies go into survival mode (fearing there's a famine), slowing our metabolism so that we burn less fuel (I talk more about this in Part One). This is why it gets harder to keep losing weight as you get closer to your goal, and is the main reason I *always* advocate exercise as part of any weight-loss plan, since exercise builds muscle, and the more muscle you have, the higher your metabolic rate. Exercise is also brilliant for self-confidence and discipline and, for some, camaraderie. **For all these reasons, continuing to exercise after you lose weight is critical to maintaining weight loss.** I go into this in more detail in Part Two.

Now when it comes to losing weight, I've always said that what you put in your mouth is way more important than how much exercise you do. So, if I had two overweight clients, one who trained like a demon but ate whatever they wanted, and another who did no exercise but tidied up their diet so that they had a weekly calorie deficit, *the non-exerciser would lose the most weight.* Yet when it comes to *maintaining* that weight over the long term, the amount of physical activity you do becomes *very important.* This is partly due to the metabolic effects of exercise, but also to its positive

I asked people about their experiences of managing weight loss in the long term, and have featured some of those stories here as case studies.

effects on mood and feelings of 'self-efficacy' (being in control of your life). Which is why I'm a major advocate of morning exercise, before 'life' gets in the way and messes up our plans. Get it done first!

A 2014 review of the role of exercise and physical activity in weight loss and maintenance by Swift and colleagues concluded that people who do more than 200 minutes of moderate to high-intensity exercise each week (around 30 minutes per day), in conjunction with a calorie-controlled diet, will not only increase their likelihood of keeping weight off but also reduce their risk factors for diabetes and heart disease. Then there's research from the National Weight Control Registry in the US, which has found that 91 per cent of successful weight maintainers do *at least* one hour of moderately intense exercise every day. Three-quarters also eat breakfast without fail and weigh themselves at least once a week.

WHY DO WE REGAIN THE WEIGHT?

When I reached out to my fitness and weight-loss community, one of the most common reasons they gave for regaining weight was being unable to exercise after an accident or injury. They told me they felt helpless and hopeless, and some of them turned to food for consolation. While I can see where they're coming from, the truth is, depending on the injury, there are always other ways to get your heart rate up and your muscles working so you can continue to enjoy both the physical and emotional benefits of exercise. That's why I've included some basic exercises and workouts in Part Five that you can do in your lounge room or the local park. I've also thrown in some simple ideas for outdoor family games – they're so much fun, and so good for the mind, body and soul.

The other major reason people gave for falling off the wagon was stress. Whether it was a job loss, a relationship breakup, illness in the family or even just moving house, many said that these life changes made it harder to find the time to exercise or to resist using alcohol/food to feel better. They would then berate themselves for being pathetic and weak, which fuelled their emotional eating.

As you know, I'm always banging on about taking responsibility for your health, but that doesn't begin with self-hatred and self-blame. It begins with acceptance: 'I am looking after myself in the best way I can.' From there you can make choices that come from a place of love, not fear. If you know that you're an emotional eater, you're going to need help dealing with stress in ways that don't involve food (I personally find that exercise is a great stress-buster). I look at those in Part Two.

If you've lost weight before, you'll already know how to set up your household and your work environment to support you. That means not having junk food in the house, even if your loved ones fight you on it. It means planning ahead when it comes to snacking and travelling. It means eating regular meals with enough protein and

When we know better, we can do better.

healthy fats to keep you feeling full. It means not letting yourself go so long between meals that the plastic-wrapped crap at service stations looks appetising. It means deciding each day to take care of *you*. If you can redesign your environment to reduce the constant temptation, then you won't need to call on willpower all the time; you will automatically make good choices out of sheer force of habit.

KEEPING IT OFF

I've always said that losing weight is a science and keeping it off is a psychology, and as our knowledge in these areas grows, we realise that the impact of both these factors on weight loss is greater than we thought. Complex factors in our biology and environment also exert powerful influences on whether we can sustain weight loss in the long term. But this doesn't mean we should despair and give up. On the contrary, we can now move forward armed with a good dose of reality. Rather than pinning our hopes on empty promises, we can focus on real solutions. **When we know better, we can do better.** And doing better means shifting our obsession with the outsides of our bodies to the insides. It means eating minimally processed, nutrient-dense foods and exercising because this makes us *feel* better and helps us to *think* better. It means reframing the way we think about ourselves, and the foods we eat.

The great thing is that you don't need to lose stacks of weight to enjoy better health. Losing as little as 5 per cent improves blood pressure and levels of circulating triglycerides and glucose – all risk factors for heart disease. In the US Diabetes Prevention Program study, people at risk for type 2 diabetes who lost just 7 per cent of their weight and exercised for about 30 minutes a day cut their risk of diabetes by nearly 60 per cent. A 2014 South Australian study of obese people with atrial fibrillation (which is a heart condition where the heart doesn't pump properly) found that 45 per cent of patients who lost 10 per cent or more of their body weight (and 22 per cent of patients who lost 3 to 9 per cent) were free from atrial fibrillation symptoms after four years without needing surgery or medication.

On the following pages I have provided you with a clear plan of action that has worked for me: a set of tools that will help you get to where you need to be. It will be challenging, but it's in these moments that you're building resilience and learning more about yourself. I hope that I can inspire you to celebrate your successes, rather than focus on your setbacks – to be kind to yourself no matter what shape you are. Even if you manage to maintain a weight loss of only a few kilos, be proud you have got this far, and know that if you are exercising every day and eating nutritious wholefoods, every cell in your body will respond with renewed vitality. You will be the best person you can be and an inspiration to everyone around you.

This year I started up again. I thought of my WHYs (as I'm doing this journey with two of my best friends and we all listed ours... this time, I'm in a good headspace). I've started walking daily over the past week but I feel so much better. I've only lost 2.7 kg but I'm going to start walking in the mornings and hope that it helps. If I push myself too much, I know I'll give up so I'm taking baby steps. I've got about 50 kg or so to lose... fingers crossed!!! Just a part of my 'why': I don't want to have to wake up to roll over in bed, I don't want my feet swelling when I sit down, I want to sit cross-legged on the floor without pain or pins and needles, I don't want my boobs and tummy all rolled into one when I sit down, I don't want to look like a bloated blown-up ball, I want my neck and chin to be two separate things, I want rings to fit my fingers, I want necklaces to fit my neck, I don't want to have to wear three-quarter pants in summer, I want to be intimate with my partner and run without jiggling and feeling absolutely disgusting and disgraceful, I don't want the judgy eyes, I don't want the whispers, I don't want to be miserable anymore, I want to do fun things, I want to have fun without alcohol, I want to wear shorts and a singlet and look good, I want to bushwalk, I want to get on a boat without thinking I'm going to slip and go thud, I want to travel, I want to go out for dinner and sit down without worrying if the chair will break, I want to have children more than anything in this world, I want to get married and feel like a beautiful bride, I don't want to hide anymore, I want to love myself, I want to LIVE.
— SPARKLING_HEART: VICKI

Mish says...

Vicki is right at the beginning of her journey. And when we are at the beginning of anything we have to allow ourselves to be beginners. Reframing our thinking, like 'I want to make a change. This is now my new way of being' takes time and patience.

I have been on a weight-loss journey and lost 35 kg and am maintaining that loss. I tried so hard in the past to lose weight but all for reasons that weren't for ME. Once I made the decision that my journey was for me and nobody else, things fell into place. I stopped restricting foods and ate to nourish my body instead. Choosing strength training over hours of cardio and just living life for me and my family instead of society's pressures and 'norms', I'm now the healthiest and fittest I have ever been. — SIOBHAN

Mish says...

A classic example of a change of headspace and, in turn, a change of environment. Siobhan made the choice for herself. My experience tells me she has routine and habit in place.

KEIRA'S STORY

CASE · · STUDY

What made you decide to lose weight in the first place? What was your WHY?

I wanted to be happy in my body, and to be healthy for myself and my family. I was struggling post-babies with lack of sleep and little reprieve from raising two young children. The program with the exercise routine was a great break away and chance for 'me time', which was fantastic and certainly a lifesaver at that time in my life.

Did you set a goal weight?

I had targets as I went along. I wasn't sure where it would end exactly. Under 85 kg, 80 kg, 75 kg, 70 kg, 68 kg, 65 kg.

Did you reach your goal weight?

I got to 66.7 kg, under my 68 kg target, but above my 65 kg target. In hindsight, I should have worked on maintaining 68 kg rather than aiming for lower.

How much weight in total did you lose?

23 kg.

How long were you able to maintain this goal weight?

Not long at all, it was very brief. I had so much fun at this time, shopping for clothes, socialising and feeling fantastic. I was happy and enjoying life.

What are the key factors that helped or hindered your ability to manage your weight?

Being so regimented in all that I did to lose the weight, with both food and exercise, affected my social life for myself and my family. It took up so much time and focus to achieve the weight loss, honestly it got boring to those around me. I didn't realise at the time, but it was limiting to my immediate family.

Life got busy with working and having young kids, and we live overseas away from our extended family and friends. It was challenging to maintain everything. I had a back injury in the gym and this slowed me down and I never really got back to the same exercise intensity again.

Over three years, I've now put all the weight back on. I've started to make positive changes to lose weight again, but am focusing on doing it slower and gently, looking after my body as I go along. My main exercise is walking and swimming and I plan to add weights back in slowly with care.

My priority is eating well (real food, reducing portions and limiting alcohol), getting good sleep every day and consistently exercising. I'm not making a big song and dance of it all, and I don't discuss it with people. I don't want my choices affecting those around me.

Mish says...

Could Keira 'reframe' her thinking? What if discipline could be considered nurturing? Building a framework through routine and habit keeps chaos at bay when life gets busy. A move overseas, away from family and friends, might be an opportunity to allow for more space for you. A time to nurture yourself.

PART ONE

WHY WE REGAIN WEIGHT

Snake-oil merchants have long known that anyone can lose weight by restricting calories, which is one reason we've seen some of the stupidest (and unhealthiest) diets in human history, such as the grapefruit diet and the cabbage soup diet. But when it comes to keeping weight off, scientists are only just beginning to understand the complex interplay of biological, behavioural and environmental factors that see most of us regain the weight.

BIOLOGICAL FACTORS

Humans are wired for survival and have evolved tightly regulated homeostatic systems to control energy metabolism. (Homeostasis, from the Greek words for 'same' and 'steady', refers to any process that helps create the stable conditions necessary for survival.) Our body weight control centre is in the hypothalamus, deep inside our brain. Its job is to process signals from the rest of the body (the pancreas, liver, muscles, gastrointestinal tract and adipose tissue) about nutrient availability and energy stores and to coordinate our appetite-controlling hormones to balance our energy intake.

The theory goes that, unlike most other animals, we have large brains that require a constant supply of glucose, plus we have relatively long pregnancies and neonatal periods, both of which meant that we evolved *very* efficient fat-storage processes. This made good sense for our nomadic ancestors, who could never be sure of the next meal, and even for early farming civilisations, who regularly experienced famine due to crop failure, natural disasters and war. Even now, adequate fat storage continues to influence our reproductive fitness, as young women who are too thin stop having periods. The upshot of all of this is that when we reduce our caloric intake over a long period (aka go on a diet) our body goes into survival mode: our metabolism slows right down to conserve energy, furiously storing fat and ramping up our appetite for carbs.

Mish says...

Michelle's honesty will allow her to move forward. She has owned that going back to her old habits has hindered her. Identifying your habits gives you the knowledge to move forward, make changes and outmaneuver foreseeable pitfalls. With more stress at work, a 'reframe' of thinking could allow her to choose which habits nurture her, give her clarity and calm the chaos. Habit and routine is a lifeline. Every day, same same.

CASE STUDY

In 2013 my sister told me she was doing your 12WBT so I thought I would give it a go. I felt very unfit, very overweight and my clothes didn't fit. I am short and weighed 72 kg. I set a goal weight of 60 kg.

I ended up losing a total of 17 kg and got to 55 kg after two rounds. I kept it off for eighteen months. The third time I lost motivation. My work hours and stress increased.

What hindered me was going back to drinking and not eating as healthy and doing less exercise. Holidays also didn't help. Doing the mindset tasks prior to the challenge was a great help, as was keeping a food diary to count calories. I would love to lose the weight and feel great and fit again, but worry about time and stress making me fail. I don't know how I did it last time. I would love to know how to maintain and not put it back on. — MICHELLE

SLOWED METABOLISM

When we're talking about losing weight, the biggest calorie-burning factor is our basal metabolic rate (BMR), which is the energy our body needs to perform the bazillion processes that keep us alive (our heart pumping blood, our lungs exchanging gases, our digestive system breaking down food, our brain processing information, our kidneys filtering our blood, etc). Our BMR accounts for 65–75 per cent of our daily calorie expenditure – that's nearly three-quarters! The remaining 15–30 per cent is accounted for by physical activity. Now that's not just going to the gym or going for a run. It's *all* of your physical activity – hanging out the washing, brushing your teeth, even scratching your butt. Your body also expends energy breaking down and storing nutrients. This is referred to as the 'thermic effect' of food and accounts for the remaining 5–10 per cent of your total daily calorie expenditure. And by the way, we burn the most calories digesting protein and the least calories digesting sugar and refined carbs – fat sits somewhere in the middle (pardon the pun).

So, if you cut your calorie intake by 300 calories per day you will gradually lose weight. This is because your body still needs the same amount of energy to keep your body functioning and moving, and so it sources this energy from stored fat. However, as we saw above, we're wired to keep some fat for emergencies, so our body *also starts breaking down protein*, which means that you're also slowly losing some lean muscle. As your lean muscle gradually reduces, so does your metabolic rate (see page 42 for more on the relationship between muscle mass and metabolism).

Moreover, our metabolism remains sluggish even after we begin to gain weight again. One recent study of fourteen contestants from the US series of *The Biggest Loser* found that all had much lower metabolic rates *six years* after the show, and that the ones who had regained the most weight had the lowest. This is why I am so adamant that when you are losing weight, you *must* retain your lean muscle by weight training and refuelling your body with protein. It is also why you need to continue to maintain muscle tone afterwards.

INCREASED APPETITE

Some people reading this will probably punch the air, saying 'I knew it!'. And yes, there is a great deal of evidence that losing weight messes with your appetite-controlling hormones, reducing circulating levels of satiety hormones such as leptin, and increasing hunger hormones such as ghrelin. These changes also persist for *at least* twelve months after you lose weight (possibly longer), even if you've started putting the weight back on.

You can see the problem here. You've lost weight and you feel fantastic, but your brain is telling you you're starving. Not only that, but you're living in what is called an 'obesogenic environment'. High-calorie, low-nutrient foods are tempting you at every turn, every second ad on TV is for takeaway food and there's an avalanche of reality TV cooking shows with shot after shot of delectable morsels sizzling in oil. Worse, our supermarkets seem to be overflowing with unhealthy processed foods that can be extremely tempting for anyone who is hungry, tired and time-poor.

Now I'm not saying that this rocket-powered appetite is experienced by everyone. In fact, one study found that these changes don't seem to occur when people lose less than 5 per cent of their body weight, suggesting that a critical level of weight loss may be needed to trigger increased appetite. But if you are someone who genuinely experiences those intense feelings of hunger, it can be a monumental effort to distract yourself from eating, especially when you also consider the other important fact about food – it stimulates brain centres involved in pleasure and reward.

Think about it. If appetite was controlled only by homeostatic mechanisms, we would eat only as much as we needed to survive, with a bit stored for a rainy day, but this is *so* not the case. The increasing prevalence of obesity and related diseases such as diabetes, cardiovascular disease and kidney disease shows that there are other factors at play. And one of those is the brain's reward circuitry. Eating activates pleasure centres in our brain via the dopaminergic system. In other words, we're also wired to respond to the sight, smell and taste of food, and these sensory inputs can be powerful enough to override the hypothalamus' homeostatic system, increasing the desire to eat even when we're full. The bad news is that this neural responsiveness to food cues increases within hours of caloric restriction.

A recent study found that people on a calorie-restricted diet not only had a greater preoccupation with the foods they were not supposed to eat, but with *all* foods, leading to stronger urges to eat more frequently and greater feelings of being out of control with their eating. This is why it is so important to have three meals a day (see page 52), along with a healthy snack or two if you really need them. It's also why drinking water is important, as our bodies can sometimes confuse thirst with hunger.

> The turning point for me was realising for a better life I had to change everything.
>
> Molly

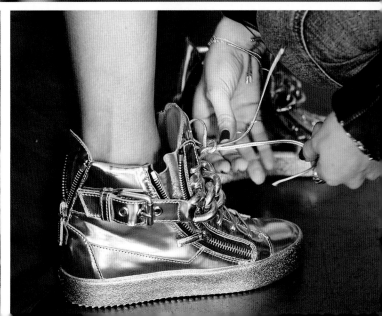

INTERVIEW WITH PROFESSOR KATHERINE SAMARAS

Now I'm not a scientist, or a doctor – I'm a fitness professional with a passion for helping people enjoy happy and healthy lives. Yes, I can read research papers and tell you what I've learned, but for this book I decided it was important to go to the source – to talk to a respected endocrinologist and researcher who devotes her life to understanding the causes, prevention and treatment of obesity and metabolic disease.

Professor Katherine Samaras is a senior staff specialist in endocrinology and metabolism at St Vincent's Hospital in Sydney and laboratory head, Clinical Obesity, Nutrition and Adipose Biology at the Garvan Institute of Medical Research. She is also the founder and director of the Australian Centre for Metabolic Health (St Vincent's Clinic) and her research is helping us to understand the connection between obesity and inflammatory diseases such as diabetes, kidney disease, heart disease and dementia.

Professor Samaras explained that everyone has a 'set point' for body weight and that this set point is partly determined by our genes (our DNA) and partly by environmental factors (food, drink, sleep, stress, etc). Once environmental factors have triggered weight gain, our hormones adjust to the new heavier weight and thereafter constantly try to keep us at that higher weight – it's our set weight point. If you have the genes for being predisposed to fast weight gain, environmental factors will trigger your weight gain faster than someone without those genes.

But Professor Samaras was emphatic that people who are genetically predisposed to gain weight really quickly are not faulty or inferior – in fact, they're the survivors. In times of famine (and until relatively recently, human beings regularly faced starvation), the fast weight gainers would have ensured that some of their community survived to create the next generation. She said that people with a high weight set point should regard themselves in a positive light – as survivors, rather than victims who have been dealt a crappy genetic hand.

I can imagine people who discover they have the genetics for obesity feeling victimised and wanting to stop playing altogether, because their genetic hand is a 'hard' one. But if we step back and view those genetics as the survivor genes, then that's not a hard hand, that's the winning hand! Although it sounds counterintuitive, the first step to changing ourselves is accepting who we are. We start from a place of love.

Yet Professor Samaras was honest about the tenacity required. People who have been very overweight and then lost the weight will need a lifetime of support and encouragement to keep the weight off. This is because their set point has been pushed higher, triggering the change that sends their appetite-controlling hormones out of whack long term. She also made the brilliant point that needing ongoing support is not a sign of weakness or failure – we don't see having help with, say, our computers or our finances as a weakness. Why should support for our health be any different?

Rather than viewing weight management as a life sentence of discipline and drudgery, Professor Samaras asks us to reframe our understanding as empowering – we know what we need to do to keep the weight off long term and it's not a chore, it's just the way it is. The truth is that formerly obese people who lose weight will not be able to loosen the reins even a little – not even for a weekly treat meal. They can have a treat meal on their birthday, or perhaps one other special occasion, but other than that, they must stick to calorie control. That may sound austere, but this is how human beings lived for millennia before fast-food chains took over our suburbs and our supermarkets overflowed with highly processed 'foods'. We'd work hard all day, mostly outdoors, and sit down to a simple meal we had grown, gathered or slain ourselves. There was only one 'special occasion' feast a year (usually at harvest time). Now we are sitting down to the calorie equivalent of a Christmas feast *every single day*, without having chopped wood, carried water or ploughed even a centimetre of land.

For those who have gained weight in the past but do not have the genetics for obesity, they too will still have to work consciously and consistently to maintain their weight loss for the long term. There truly is no such thing as a free lunch! These people will find they're able to have a treat meal once a week, or a glass of wine maybe once or twice a week or the occasional dessert – but they will need to stick to calorie control around that, as a long-term matter of habit.

Professor Samaras recognises that weight issues for some people are brought on by stress. This is because eating triggers the release of serotonin and endorphins, so we eat more to feel better. She says that we need to rehabilitate our relationship to food. If this sounds like you, then understanding this about yourself is an important first step; the next important step is having a strategy ready to go when you feel this coming on.

At its core, food is fuel – we need to find our feel-good fix in other ways, to think of other activities that elevate our mood. For me it's exercise. For others, it might be meditation, going to a concert or a theatre performance, or reading a really good book!

She also made the crucial point that women who are overweight before and during pregnancy are setting up their unborn child for a life of weight and health issues. Recent research has found that women who are overweight at conception or who gain excessive weight in pregnancy will not only have a newborn with a higher birth weight, but their children have a much greater risk of being overweight or obese by the time they are at school. If you can eat well and keep your weight gain to 7–10 kg in pregnancy, you will 'wire' your child's genes for the best chance for a long and healthy life.

OUR GENES

Scientists are working hard to understand how our genes and environment interact to cause obesity, as this info could be crucial for future prevention and treatment. So far, however, genetic factors can only explain a proportion of obesity cases, and most of these are rare genetic conditions. The reality is that environmental factors (aka poor nutrition and lack of exercise) have a far greater influence on our body weight. One 2016 study found that obese people who carried one of the obesity genes (the FTO gene) responded equally well to diet and exercise interventions as obese people who didn't carry the gene. Scientists also know from twin studies that people with these genes do not necessarily become overweight, and that a healthy lifestyle can prevent gene expression. **So, when people tell me they have 'fat genes', I love to reply that yes, genetics may load the gun, but it's environment that pulls the trigger.** This is empowering news, as it means everyone has a chance to improve their health and wellbeing.

Another possible genetic factor involves fat cells (adipocytes). After we lose weight, the fat cells in our body become primed to take up and store energy (fat), and are able to do so more rapidly and efficiently than they did before we lost weight. However, the location of fat cells in our body (something partly determined by our genes) may have more influence on whether we become unhealthy when we are overweight.

Starting in the 1960s, some researchers began to notice that not everyone who was obese had high blood triglycerides or insulin sensitivity, meaning they lacked the risk factors for heart disease and diabetes. Studies showed that the key difference between obese people who were healthy and those who were unhealthy was *where* they stored their fat. Those who were metabolically healthy had *half* the visceral (intra-abdominal) fat of those who were not. They also exercised more. So, although we may have no control over where our bodies choose to store fat, we *do* have control over what we eat and how active we are, which can mitigate the risk factors for disease.

> Genetic factors can only explain a proportion of obesity cases.

PREGNANCY

Weight gain during pregnancy has got to be one of the most common factors my clients give for becoming overweight and not being able to shift the extra kilos. Yet body fat is *super* important, not only to support the developing baby, but to see mums through the months of breastfeeding. In fact, a BMI of 20–25 is considered optimal for pregnancy. (Most women actually stop menstruating if their BMI falls to 17 or 18 because their bodies aren't convinced that there's enough stored energy to see them through pregnancy, let alone breastfeeding. It's our body's way of safeguarding us and our babies.) But too much fat can be a problem, too. Recent studies have found that if you begin your pregnancy overweight, you are not only more likely to put on more weight during your pregnancy, but you're also going to find it harder to lose that weight after your baby is born.

Most women put on a couple of kilos in the first trimester, and the weight gain from that point forward is usually evenly spread at around half a kilo a week with perhaps a little more towards the end. Importantly, your weight gain should be slower if you are overweight. This means that for a woman with a BMI of 30 or more (technically obese), total weight gain throughout the pregnancy should pretty much be accounted for by the weight of the baby, the amniotic fluid he or she is bobbing around in, and any additional weight due to lactation.

Exercise, of course, is my number-one tip for shedding post-pregnancy weight (that and clean eating). Walking is an excellent starting point, because you can take your baby with you and you can do it anywhere. Carry him or her in a sling, front pack or backpack – it's reassuring for your baby to be so close to you and the weight increases your load and calorie expenditure. Of course, always consult your doctor before starting any exercise after pregnancy.

MIDDLE AGE

As we age, we lose muscle tone, not only because we live a more sedentary lifestyle, but also because the production of hormones that support muscle growth slows down. Unfortunately for all you blokes out there, your testosterone levels start slipping from around the age of thirty at the rate of about 1 per cent a year, or even more if you have any testicular damage. But before us girls start getting too smug, there's a ton of research showing that as our oestrogen levels fall, so do our metabolic rates and with them our calorie-burning ability. So, we can be eating the *same* number of calories and even doing the same amount of exercise as we did before we reached middle age, but we still put on weight. The only thing that actually increases is our appetite – seriously! Appetite-controlling cells (POMC neurons) are progressively damaged and killed off by free radicals as we get older, so while our hunger neurons are still relaying the message that we're hungry, the ones relaying the message that our hunger is satisfied become impaired, and we're up there helping ourselves to seconds. Falling oestrogen levels also mess with our glucose tolerance – how our bodies cope with sugar. As you approach middle age, you can start to take into account how some of these changes will affect your lifestyle and how to mitigate them.

MY PREGNANCY

Once Steve and I had made the decision to have a baby, I swung into action around my nutrition. I've always had a good wholefood diet, but I started upping things like folate and fish oils, reducing alcohol and pumping up my veggies. My focus was on being in the best possible health I could be.

When we found out we were pregnant, I was blown away. Wow! I'm forty-four and we conceived naturally! I suddenly had an even greater respect for my body. It made me determined to look after myself and my baby.

Within a couple of weeks the exhaustion hit me. At the time, I'd just started filming *The Biggest Loser*, and by every afternoon I could barely stand up. The first three months were the hardest – trying to keep myself propped up as well as keep my growing belly under wraps. Thank god for my puffer vest!

I watched with a mixture of fascination and awe as my body changed and my fitness slowly lapsed. Hell, I was puffing going up a set of stairs! As a professional trainer, I can't remember the last time I'd experienced that, and it gave me more insight into what it was like for my clients. But I wasn't too concerned about putting on weight. I was just way too excited about having a baby growing inside me! It overrode any worries about my body changing. And I really loved my belly. I felt strangely proud of it, as though I was the only woman on the planet who'd ever had a baby! And yes, I actually miss it.

My focus was on being in the best possible health I could be.

That said, I knew that the best thing I could do was eat well – eating for double the nutrition rather than eating for two – along with getting plenty of sleep and continuing training. I still did my weights and cardio, but they were a lot more passive and I continued to scale them back each week. Being active throughout my pregnancy allowed me to maintain most of my strength and fitness while keeping my head in a happy, positive place. In the past, women were discouraged from exercising because it was believed it could trigger premature delivery. But there is plenty of research to show that this is simply not true. In fact, studies show that exercise is valuable for the health of mum and bub during pregnancy, birth and post-delivery. Provided you have your doctor's clearance, I say go for it. You simply tone it down week by week as you get bigger.

For my height and stature, I knew that putting on 12–16 kilograms would be about right for me. I ended up putting on 15 kilos, which I felt was a great result.

The birth of my son, Axel, was the most amazing thing I have ever experienced and I knew that I wanted to soak him up for weeks and weeks, so getting back into shape was furthest from my mind. I just wanted to spend time with him. For the first few weeks, I simply went walking with him in the pram, and that was awesome. I waited six weeks before working on getting back my core strength. If you have any complications with your pregnancy or birth, any exercise needs to be discussed with your doctor and a professional physio or chiro. My team were amazing and super switched on about taking care of core strength and, well, all my lady bits! Kegel exercises, ladies!

The birth of my son, Axel, was the most amazing thing I have ever experienced.

Having maintained some regular exercise throughout my pregnancy, I feel sure it assisted my journey back to physical fitness. Even so, it was a full year before I felt I was completely back. Of course, I know that my body will never be the same again after having a baby. My belly might not be quite as strong or as flat. I've lost muscle tone, and hormones have changed my skin, too. But so what! I'm incredibly proud of myself and my body. I will continue to eat well, train consistently and maintain a positive outlook. And that's called taking care of me!

ENVIRONMENTAL FACTORS

As I mentioned earlier, pretty much every feature of our modern way of life promotes weight gain (our 'obesogenic environment'). 'Big Food' companies use slick marketing to sell us high-calorie, low-nutrient 'food' that some researchers claim is slowly killing us. We live in a world of automation, effortless transportation and static entertainment, all of which set us up to move less and less. Our buildings are designed for us to get around in them quickly with a minimum of effort. Then there's the effect of poor-quality sleep, stress and other psychological factors, such as our expectation to be happy 24/7 and to have everything we want immediately (instant gratification). Let's look at some of these in more detail.

REDUCED REWARD

When I reached out to my fitness and weight-loss community, several people told me that one of the reasons it was hard to maintain weight loss was because they'd lost the motivation to keep going. They missed the sense of accomplishment they got when they saw the number on the scales drop, or when they first went shopping for smaller clothes, or when friends and family made positive comments on their achievements. Once they reached their goal weight, or had settled for whatever loss they achieved, they no longer felt the buzz of positive feedback so it was harder to continue with the meal and exercise regimen.

This is why it is *so* important to have support, whether it be training with a buddy, having your family eat the same nutritious wholefood meals, seeing your doctor regularly for health checkups, or connecting with an online health and fitness community (see page 46). It's also why it is important to look at any emotional factors that might be interfering with your health goals (see page 47).

> Pretty much every feature of our modern way of life promotes weight gain.

CRAP FOOD

Practically everywhere we go – sports grounds, cinemas, petrol stations, shopping centres, gyms and even *hospitals* – high-crap, low-nutrient food is shoved under our noses. And let's not mince words: the vast majority of this so-called food is crap because it contains refined flour, sugar, preservatives and dodgy oils that increase shelf life at the lowest cost to the manufacturer. And our supermarkets are generally no different. Back in the 1970s the average supermarket had around 4000 food items; now it has 80,000 items, many of which are manufactured foods based on refined wheat flour, sugar and seed (vegetable) oils. So, while it may look like we have more to choose from, it's a case of same shit, different bucket.

JILL'S STORY

I'm a single woman in her late fifties living in a country town. I joined a few years ago now with the goal to lose about 20 kg. This was because I really didn't like the way I looked. I had also been diagnosed about twelve months before as pre-diabetic and needed to take better care of myself. I'm not a diet junkie, although I had tried Weight Watchers some years before and lost quite a lot of weight then (which I subsequently put on again!). From WW I learned to ensure I ate three meals a day – not miss brekkie – so that did change one aspect of my lifestyle. I put the weight on again because I started eating too much – comfort food, I think.

I heard about 12WBT from a friend and had been watching her weight loss for a few months. She was a great ambassador! I started as my New Year's Resolution and really appreciated the program – from the 'getting my head right' and setting up the pantry, to the recipes and exercise plans. I didn't follow either of them to the tee – I built some of the exercises around a program of pilates twice a week, swimming 1 km twice a week, and walking daily. Stuck religiously to the 1200 calories – LOOOOVED some of the recipes, but certainly not all. Once again, I made it work to suit me. I weighed myself regularly and frequently. I noticed the weight loss on the scales, of course, but reality hit home when my clothing started to be too baggy to wear comfortably!

I really got into walking, listening to podcasts and wearing a monitor to keep track of heart rate and calories burnt! Over about a twelve-month period I ended up completing three 12 km City to Surfs (in Sydney, Melbourne and Perth), having never done one before. Oh, and the local Margaret River to Prevally run. I walked them all, but not slowly! Quite proud of myself really! Then I injured my groin, probably through striding out too much when I was walking fast, which gave me an excuse not to exercise as much as I did. I went on holidays, got out of routine and I put on the weight probably due to eating too much.

I have pretty constantly been renewing my membership to keep the recipes and try to gain inspiration. I noticed the changes to the food over the years with the best innovation (for me) being the single meals. I hate eating the same food two days in a row. Cooking is something I enjoy.

My aim next time I do this is to lose the weight – then focus on how to keep it there! The second part is going to be my biggest challenge!

Mish says...

Jill had set up her environment to work for her. She was in the groove, and loving it! Injury can be a setback OR an opportunity to try new things. With a lower body injury, it's a chance to spend time on upper body strength or doing the stretching and mobility work that often gets neglected. Perhaps even trying something new, like swimming. All of which allows you to stay in the groove.

For me, healthy foods are minimally processed and high in nutrients – aka veggies, fruit, wholegrain breads and cereals, healthy fats like olive oil, and lean protein. But I'm also a realist, and whilst I would love us all to have the capabilities to cook from scratch every night of the week, I know it doesn't always happen. That's why I created my Delicious Nutritious range – to give people the option of eating fast, great-quality nutritious meals for those occasional times when life just gets in the way.

Sugar and high-starch carbs

The body metabolises foods at different rates, and simple carbohydrates (including sugar and starches) are broken down the quickest. Protein is metabolised the slowest, thereby expending the most energy. Fats are metabolised after carbs and before protein, and are converted directly to – you guessed it – fat. But it is far better to eat healthy fats like olive oil, avocado and nuts than foods containing sugar and/or refined grains.

Here's how it works. Anything we consume that the body is able to break down into glucose is metabolised by every organ and tissue in the body (glucose is our brain's preferred energy source). But too much glucose in the blood is toxic (and can lead to kidney damage, blindness and even limb amputation), so the pancreas secretes a hormone called insulin, which moves excess glucose from the blood into the liver and muscles (where it is stored as glycogen). When those storage areas are full, any excess glucose is converted to and stored as fat. This process ensures that the glucose levels in our blood are not at toxic levels. (It is this process that goes seriously awry when we consistently consume too much of anything that can be broken down to glucose, resulting in too much glucose left in the blood. Hello toxicity, and its terrible consequences of kidney damage, type 2 diabetes, etc.)

If we consume a stack of sugar in one hit, the pancreas releases a stack of insulin in response, to cope with all the glucose. When the insulin finishes its job, usually 90–120 minutes after eating, we get a sudden drop in blood glucose, which in turn triggers our hunger hormones (and also makes us feel a bit flat and lacking in energy). So even though we really don't *need* to eat or drink anything, our body's hunger hormones are telling us we *want* it – setting us up for a steady weight regain.

You might think you're safe if you steer clear of sugar in any form, and you'd be right. Unfortunately, other carbohydrates have similar effects. Refined or highly processed grains (e.g. the white flour in bread, cakes, pasta and noodles) have had the outer husk (bran) and germ removed (the bits with vitamins, minerals and fibre), which means the starches are more rapidly converted to glucose. The same goes for starchy root vegetables, which are also quickly broken down to glucose (especially if you peel them). This is the reason I have always preferred wholefoods, as they not only contain more vitamins and minerals, but also more fibre (see page 30), which is awesome for digestive health and immune function among other things.

Too much glucose in the blood is toxic.

Dodgy oils

For decades we've been told that saturated fats (butter, cream, animal fats, coconut oil) are evil, mostly because they are more readily stored as body fat and less easily used as fuel, and we've been advised to replace them with polyunsaturated ones (seed/vegetable oils). But while it's true that eating too much saturated fat does have some correlation with obesity and heart disease, more and more studies are showing that eating too much polyunsaturated oil may be worse.

There are two polyunsaturated fatty acids (PUFAs) that we have to get from our diet (the body can't make them): omega-3 and omega-6 (linoleic acid). These are important for normal growth and development, and for healthy brain function (our brains are actually 60 per cent fat). Yet the amount we need is very small – about half a teaspoon of each per day. Also, the balance is critical. If we get *way* more omega-6 than omega-3 (and some researchers estimate that we're eating more than twenty times as much omega-6), it creates a chronic imbalance believed to be a contributing factor in the rise of cardiovascular disease, autoimmune diseases such as arthritis, allergies and even cancer. The biochemistry is complex, but basically omega-6 fatty acids are more unstable than saturated or monounsaturated fats, and can easily oxidise to form harmful compounds in the body, contributing to inflammation and disease. Also – and here's the kicker for people trying to manage their weight – studies show that diets high in omega-6 (and in Australia, we're eating eight times as much omega-6 as omega-3) are correlated with increased fasting blood glucose, fasting insulin and insulin resistance.

You could cover a footy field with the research on which fats are associated with poor health, no doubt partly because Big Food, Big Ag and Big Pharma have a lot to lose if we turn away from oils super high in omega-6 (e.g. canola, sunflower, safflower, corn, cottonseed and soybean). I've always preferred to stick to fats that haven't had the bejesus processed out of them (e.g. cold-pressed olive and macadamia oil, and very occasionally coconut oil or butter). Plus, I just don't eat deep-fried food, or store-bought biscuits, cakes, pies, pastry, dressings, etc, which is where you find most PUFAs and, incidentally, the dodgiest fats of all – trans fats. These guys are partially hydrogenised PUFAs that are solid at room temperature and severely mess up the balance between 'bad' and 'good' cholesterol (see page 30).

I can't say what made me start, I just remember sitting at a cafe with the usual burger, chips and Coke and looking at it and saying I can't do this anymore.

Megan

> ### CHOLESTEROL
>
> Just in case you hadn't heard – our body needs cholesterol. It's used to make cell membranes, the hormones oestrogen and testosterone, vitamin D and the bile acids that help us to digest fat. About 80 per cent of the body's cholesterol is produced by the liver, while the rest comes from our diet (mainly red meat, poultry, fish, eggs and dairy products).
>
> Cholesterol is carried in the bloodstream by two main kinds of lipoproteins: low-density lipoproteins (LDL) and high-density lipoproteins (HDL). The low-density ones carry the cholesterol *from* the liver to the rest of the body, while the high-density ones carry excess cholesterol *back* to the liver for removal.
>
> LDL cholesterol is called 'bad' cholesterol because it is deposited along the inside of artery walls. Over time, this builds up to form a thick plaque that narrows the arteries and decreases blood flow through the narrowed area, setting the scene for cardiovascular disease (aka heart attacks and strokes). Luckily, the HDL ('good') cholesterol is the one that's been extracted from the artery walls and is on its way back to the liver for disposal. So, if you have more good cholesterol than bad, it will help protect you against heart disease and stroke. Bottom line – eat more fruit and veggies, less junk and processed foods and you'll be well on your way to improving your cholesterol levels.

Low-fibre foods

Fibre is the name given to the indigestible carbs in the plants we eat (fruit, veggies, grains, legumes, nuts and seeds). While we can't digest fibre, the gut bacteria in our colons can, and they thrive on it, which is great because these guys play an essential role not only in the health of our digestive system, but also our immune system and even our moods. Recent studies have found that many gut bacteria can manufacture special proteins (peptides) that are very similar to hunger-regulating hormones, which means that they may be able to influence our eating behaviour.

Unfortunately, many of us simply don't get enough fibre in our diet, which has some pretty bad knock-on effects for our health. Fibre bulks our stools, and draws water into the colon to soften them. This helps prevent and relieve bowel problems such as constipation, haemorrhoids, diverticular disease and some cases of irritable bowel syndrome. Fibre has also been shown to reduce circulating levels of LDL cholesterol and thus our risk of heart disease, and to help prevent bowel cancer. It also helps with weight management, since it takes longer to break down and pass through the gut, which means we feel fuller for longer.

Best of all, fibre from varied natural sources encourages a more diverse gut microbiome, upping our chances of staying healthy. Having fewer gut bug species is a common feature of obesity, inflammatory bowel disease and other conditions. Plus, there's evidence that a diverse microbiome can better resist invasive species like

Salmonella or *Clostridium difficile*. And what's the best way to encourage diversity? You guessed it – by eating as many different kinds of veggies, fruit, legumes, nuts, seeds and wholegrains as you can, along with some cheese and yoghurt (if you can tolerate dairy) and fermented foods such as sauerkraut and kefir.

STRESS

When we are under stress, our adrenal gland pumps out adrenaline (the 'fight or flight' hormone that elevates our heart rate, blood pressure and breathing in readiness for action), and cortisol, which is involved in glucose metabolism and blood-sugar maintenance (to supply the energy we need) as well as inflammatory response and immune function.

Unlike adrenaline, which is only produced in short bursts, cortisol can be produced long term. And one of the things an elevated cortisol level does is to increase abdominal fat. From a survival point of view, this emergency fat storage is designed to keep a person alive if they have to endure harsh or physically demanding conditions for long periods. The problem is, we're leading sedentary lives (driving cars and sitting in offices) and much of the stress is in our heads. Our modern way of life means that our cortisol level gets pumped up so many times during our busy day that it doesn't get much chance to return to normal, and most of us aren't burning any of the extra fat that's being stored in the process. This is another reason to exercise every day – it's not only brilliant for burning calories, but also for helping manage stress.

> One of the things an elevated cortisol level does is increase abdominal fat.

POOR SLEEP

How long we sleep each night has a profound effect on our weight for many reasons. If we stay up late and get up early, and sleep poorly in between, our bodies don't get to do all the important cell repair work they need. Plus, we can't concentrate and have crap reaction times, which all adds up to stress on the body, with the knock-on effect of depressing our metabolic rate and encouraging weight regain.

Also, when we don't get enough sleep, our bodies are wired to seek out more energy to cope with the extra hours we are awake. In fact, researchers have found that with shorter sleep duration, subjects show a marked decrease in circulating levels of the satiety hormone leptin and an increase in appetite-stimulating ghrelin. The problem is, this increase in appetite is way out of proportion to the additional calories we need, and many people also report a craving for carbs. In the US, population studies show that weight gain is lowest among people who sleep six–eight hours a night and highest among those who sleep less than six hours or more than eight hours.

KAREN'S STORY

I joined 12WBT in early 2012 after watching my workmate become one of your very first 12WBT champions. She'd shed a huge amount of weight and totally transformed her health and her attitude. I was inspired!

I didn't have as much to lose, but I too had a remarkable journey on this program and lost 14 kg to bring me down to 62 kg – the weight I was as a teenager! And my fitness was awesome – I actually ran the Puffing Billy Fun Run (13.6 km of hills), something I never dreamed I'd do.

Since then the weight has crept back on and my fitness has slid away. I'm now back at 74 kg and miserable. This is despite several attempts to shift it, including signing up to 12WBT again and again, each time with high hopes and dedication that slowly fades.

I've come to understand that maintaining a lower weight requires constant effort and hard work. And I mean *constant*. And sometimes I just don't have enough energy to function in *life* and keep up that effort to maintain weight at the same time.

I believe my downslide (maybe better phrased 'upslide'?) was fuelled by a number of factors:

- I lost more weight than I needed to, and so I took the foot off the pedal, letting the portion sizes creep up and the occasional unhealthy snack sneak in.
- My habits started changing when I moved house in late 2012. I was no longer able to get to the small-group training I'd been doing and couldn't find a replacement that was anywhere near as enjoyable. I was also too far from my fitness-inclined friends. I started working out alone instead, and I started skipping workouts.
- In late 2012 there was a major incident at my workplace that was very stressful. My focus shifted from dealing with the grief that surrounded this incident rather than my own health.
- I fell while ice skating and injured my back, ruling out more of the workouts that I enjoy, such as running and body-step class.
- The following year I became ill, and was diagnosed with chronic fatigue syndrome. Again, I had to scale back the exercise. As I recovered, the doctor recommended swimming or cycling, both of which I dislike so I didn't stick with them.

One thing I learned on 12WBT was the link between diet and exercise. The more I did my workouts the more I looked forward to light and healthy meals – somehow those unhealthy options just lost their appeal. In hindsight, I believe that the interruptions to my fitness regime plus the other stresses in my life worked together to increase my appetite and cravings.

I have moved back to an inner-Melbourne suburb and I am looking for another group training opportunity. I know I have to find a rhythm that works for me. With that said, and my back feeling fine, I'm off for a Sunday afternoon slow run...

Mish says...

Karen, your story resonates with me – you had your routines and habits and were kicking goals! You are so right when you say that keeping your fitness and health on track in what can be a chaotic life does require consistency. But let's look at it like this – routines and habits are a rock to cling to when life throws grenades at you. Something that will continue forever. As you said, find your rhythm.

CHILDHOOD INFLUENCES

More and more research suggests that the type of food we eat during pregnancy plays an important role in our unborn child's life. Studies have linked fatty, sugary diets in overweight mothers to the development of obesity, diabetes and even behavioural disorders in their offspring.

During pregnancy, *you* are helping to establish the blueprint of your child's physiological development. So, the next time someone tells you that you should be 'eating for two' when you're steering your pregnant self away from the greasy fries and towards the chicken salad, knee them in the groin for me, would you? If you need to, use the power of positive language. Replace 'eating for two' with 'eating for double the nutrition' and you'll be okay.

Of course, your influence goes way beyond pregnancy. Population studies show that babies who are breastfed for more than three months are less likely to develop obesity as adolescents compared with infants who are breastfed for less than three months. (But please be aware that this connection is not causal – bottle-feeding your baby does not 'cause' obesity! So, don't feel guilty if you can't breastfeed.)

Also, children don't begin to develop fat cells until the age of six, but overweight children start developing them from the age of two, and continue to do so until the end of puberty. So, while the *number* of fat cells remains constant in adulthood (they enlarge when we put weight on and shrink when we lose it), an overweight child can be burdened with up to 50 per cent more fat cells than other children.

The message here is loud and clear. Feed your growing children nutrient-rich wholefoods (no deep-fried, salty, sugary junk) or you will be setting them up for a lifetime of weight and health issues and all the heartache, frustration and emotional roller-coaster baggage that comes with them.

Mish says...

As a parent, Nicole's story really hit me, and it should give all us parents pause for thought about the eating habits we are handing down to our kids.

CASE · STUDY

Before 12WBT, I was simply eating too much food and not moving enough. I had grown up in a family of big eaters and while most of what we ate wasn't unhealthy, the portions were just too big. It was what I had grown up with and was all I knew so when I moved out of home, I continued living the same way. The 12WBT recipes really helped me understand that you can fill up with vegetables and less meat/protein and carbs. I was also exercising but I don't think I was working out effectively or enough. Simply going for a walk every day and doing the odd gym class is not enough to stay healthy. — NICOLE

PART TWO

SEVEN HABITS FOR LONG-TERM WEIGHT MANAGEMENT

If you have lost weight before, you'll know how good you feel when you eat well and exercise. This is because your body responds immediately when you switch to a nutritious wholefood diet: your good gut bugs will start to take charge, which assists digestion, immune function and even your mood; and your tastebuds will start making tiny changes to the way you appreciate food, meaning you can ditch the habit of smothering your meals in salty, sugary sauces.

The same thing happens when you have a workout – all of your body's cells respond instantaneously. And the more you stick with a regular exercise and activity regime, the greater the benefits. Your muscles get stronger (helping you burn calories faster), your heart and lung function improves and even your bones increase in density. Plus, exercise does wonders for your mood – even your brain functions better after a good workout!

In this section, I want to explore in more detail the habits that will help you maintain a healthy weight. The key is consistency – making each of these daily habits that you do without thinking and, more importantly, without attacking yourself if you trip up. Because life will throw you curve balls. That's a given. The trick is to think of the curve balls as wakeup calls to stop you drifting into complacency.

Good food and fitness are as normal
as brushing my teeth and breathing.

Renee

1 REFRAME YOUR THINKING

When it comes to maintaining a healthy weight, there are no quick fixes. Rather, it's going to take a sustained and measured approach, gradually replacing old habits with new ones that become a way of life.

In my experience, people with a 'I want it all and I want it now' mentality tend to charge into their weight-loss journey without any preparation, setting unrealistic goals and implementing super strict diet and exercise plans that are simply unsustainable in the long term. These guys are more likely to chuck the whole thing in and go back to unhealthy eating even if they have just a single lapse.

So be aware that your long-term outcome will be affected by your mindset from the get-go, and with this in mind I'd like to help you **reframe** the way you think about health and exercise. How about this: instead of seeing your efforts to maintain a healthy weight as a lifelong struggle, switch it around and see them as the ultimate empowerment – a lifelong commitment to yourself.

CHOOSE YOUR WORDS, SET YOUR GOALS

When I ask people what they want to achieve health-wise, they often say, 'I don't want to be 100 kg anymore' or 'I don't want to feel sick and tired' or 'I want to look in the mirror and not hate myself'. The problem is our minds only hear the words '100 kg', 'sick', 'tired' and 'hate myself', which serve to reinforce the negative-thought pathways that trigger associated feelings of worthlessness, anger and sadness. We then reach for high-calorie foods to help us feel better (remember that sugar and fat can activate pleasure centres in the brain), which leads to feelings of guilt and remorse, and we're stuck in that negative feedback loop.

So, start with specific, measurable, achievable, realistic and time-based (S.M.A.R.T.) goals:

- I want to be able to jog for 5 km without stopping by the end of three months.
- I want to make my own lunch to take to work every day except Wednesday.
- I want to do ten full push-ups on my toes by the end of twelve months.
- I want to drop down one jeans size by the end of six months.

Thoughts lead to words lead to actions – reframe your thoughts so they lift you up rather than drag you down.

CHALLENGE YOUR EXCUSES

Before starting a program, I get people to list all of the excuses they might come up with for not exercising or for eating crap food. This mental preparation is super important and, in my experience, the key to staying on track while you learn helpful new habits.

So be totally honest. Write down every single 'the-dog-ate-my-homework' excuse you can think of for why you can't exercise, why you can't cook, why you can't eat breakfast, why you have to eat a block of chocolate, etc. And when you have all these excuses written down, cross out the ridiculous ones (come on – some of them are ridiculous!), and then find alternative action plans for the ones that are left.

For example:

- 'I can't exercise today because it is raining.' = 'I can wear a spray jacket, and when I get hot I can tie it around my waist' or 'I can train inside with one of my exercise DVDs.'

- 'I can't say no to my colleague's birthday cake – it will look rude.' = 'I can cover my plate with a serviette and quietly put it down somewhere inconspicuous.'

- 'My kids want McDonald's and I don't have time to make different meals.' = 'I am the adult and in charge of the food in this house so I'm serving spaghetti and meatballs for the kids and zuchetti and meatballs for me.'

- 'I've had a really stressful day and I need wine to relax.' = 'I'm going to punch out 50 squats and then treat myself to sparkling mineral water with a squeeze of lemon juice, a sprig of mint and some ice cubes.'

Being able to challenge your excuses is liberating, and it's actually kind of fun. Plus, researchers have found that people with a 'growth mindset' (a more flexible thinking style where they're open to trying different options) have a greater chance of maintaining weight loss than those with a 'fixed mindset' (a more dichotomous 'all or nothing' thinking style). Which one are you?

I go to the gym early while everyone in the house is still sleeping. No time left during the day to make excuses – I'm already done before breakfast time!

Aimee

COCO GIRL'S STORY

There was not just one thing that made me decide to lose weight. Many people have one significant WHY – I had 700! So many different moments that I didn't want to experience again, so many feelings that I didn't want to feel again, so many uncomfortable situations that I didn't want to find myself in again. All of these things rolled together gave me the will and desire to actually make it happen.

I set a goal weight because I'm a huge numbers girl when it comes to planning and goal-setting. Numbers drive me so much. But I'm also realistic and understanding that all of the planning and effort in the world can't dictate what our bodies will end up doing. I'm aware that my 'number' may change as I get closer to it, and I'm okay with that. I wasn't in the beginning, though. I was determined and stubborn and believed I needed to reach that number. But I've learnt a lot along the way, and have adjusted the All Important Official Goal Number a few times to make it more realistic, healthy and attainable.

I haven't reached my goal weight yet. I lost exactly 50 kg (to the exact gram – 50.0 kg!), which was only about 15 kg away from my goal. As soon as I reached the 50 kg mark, I started going up. How long was I able to maintain the weight that I reached? Hours. Literally, hours. 50 kg was such a huge milestone for me, and as soon as I reached it, on the day, I loosened the reins. Unfortunately, I loosened them too much and for too long, and three years later I'm higher than when I began.

There were so many things that helped me lose weight. Being a member of 12WBT in the good ol' days was probably the biggest part of it. Having that community around me and having opportunities to meet up in person every twelve weeks was probably the number-one driving factor that got me through. Day in, day out, I was surrounding myself – online and in person – by people just like me, and that made a difference like no other. I always had things to look forward to in regards to my weight-loss journey – it was exciting and next-level, which inspired me and motivated me more than I can express. As soon as the community stopped (changed), so did my weight loss.

The other main factor was, of course, making the decision to change. You can have all the support and tools in the world, but unless you actually want to change, it's not going to happen.

Blogging about my journey, sharing my story on social media, counting calories, focusing on my mindset, learning more about nutrition, discovering a love of running, meal prepping, having 'calorie-free days', finding a bootcamp that I loved and tracking my journey in my own personal ways were also significant factors in my success.

Mish says...

I have a story I often tell my clients. If I had a fairy wand and could transform you to the size or weight you always wanted, what would change? The answer? Nothing. You would still continue to do the same things. So it's better to nurture yourself by eating healthily and exercising consistently, rather than just for a period of time. Coco has learnt so much about herself. Dialling back the drive of numbers and instead focusing on a regular routine that works for her. Routine and habits, they give us so much.

FIND OTHER WAYS TO DEAL WITH STRESS

One of the main reasons my fitness and weight-loss community gave for not continuing with a healthy diet and exercise plan was stress, whether that was due to illness, changing jobs, moving house or fluctuations in financial circumstances.

As we saw earlier, stress plays an important role in long-term energy homeostasis. When the brain perceives a threat (whether real or imagined), our stress hormones signal the body to store energy (and crave sugar and fat) so that we can survive whatever disaster is in store. In evolutionary terms, it was best if this fat was stored in our midsection so it could be more easily accessed by our heart, lungs and brains (no point storing it in our ankles!). Indeed, hundreds of studies have shown that stress is associated with abdominal obesity and weight gain. In one study of 5000 twin pairs, higher levels of stress were correlated with greater weight gain over a six-year period.

But what is stress? And why do some people show incredible resilience in the face of adversity, while others fall apart when their goldfish dies? If you think about it, stress is what happens when life doesn't turn out the way we planned (it rains when we want to ride to work; we get locked out of the car; we lose our job; our partner dumps us, etc). I believe it's resilience that sees us through these times. Resilience is the ability to accept what has happened and to bounce back with renewed energy, and is built when you start taking responsibility for who you are, your life and your actions. This is a practised skill, a virtue which requires consistent consideration. Obviously, many genetic and environmental factors influence our resilience, including our personality, our prenatal and childhood experiences, any illness or injury we experience and whether or not we have strong connections with family, friends and community. Yet, even if all of these factors would seem to be working against us, we can still handle stress with the right mindset.

> Stress is what happens when life doesn't turn out the way we planned.

Recognise your triggers

When you feel the urge to do something that you know is unhealthy, visualise a big stop sign (or a giant remote control with a big pause button) and just pause for a second. What are you feeling? What thoughts and images are going through your head (as you reach for the chocolate/wine/ciggies) – 'I'm a failure', 'He doesn't love me', 'My partner never listens to me', 'It's my fault', 'I'm ugly', 'No one wants to talk to me'?

It doesn't have to be a big deal – just pause, and notice the connection between your thoughts and feelings. Because I'm telling you now, it's these thoughts that are the triggers for your old habits, and recognising them (before you take action) is the first step to making lasting changes to your self-care. Here are some examples:

- If you feel sad and lonely, rather than reaching for the chocolate, reach for your phone and call a friend instead.
- If you feel down because you believe you're a failure, instead of opening the wine, open a notebook and write down three things you did well today, and then go do something around the house that you've been putting off and add it to the list!
- If you feel angry at your partner, rather than rip into a cigarette, rip outside for a run to get those feel-good endorphins racing. The added benefit here is that you get time out to calm down and you can come back and talk calmly to your partner about whatever it was that caused the anger in the first place.

Every time you choose a healthy option, you will be strengthening a new neural pathway, and the old one will slowly fade away.

Mish says...

I love that Hollie mentions 'owning' a day where the wheels fall off, and moving on. It happens. She's learnt things about herself, like how to say no. And she understands that it's a long life, and it's all about consistency. Nice one!

CASE STUDY

I've now lost 51 kg, slowly but surely. I think the most important factors in weight loss are focusing on yourself mentally, changing habits and recognising self-sabotage. I used to have a bad day food-wise and just give up, instead of just owning that day and starting again the next day. I think it's really important to have supportive people around you and know how to be able to say no to dinners and cake and such (which is so much harder than it seems!). Also about focusing on non-weight goals rather than becoming obsessed with the number on the scales! I had a few people in my life that loved me but would sabotage me by saying 'Oh you've been doing so well, that piece of cake won't hurt', but it did! Standing up for myself was the hardest thing I have ever done! Meeting like-minded people in the forums [12WBT member chatrooms] and Facebook groups really helped too. And having a balanced life and doing stuff for just ME really made a difference. I know I will always struggle with my weight but I do like myself now... slowly learning to love myself! Thanks for letting me ramble on. xox — HOLLIE

EXERCISE *EVERY SINGLE DAY*

The human body is designed to move – we actually have 206 bones and around 700 skeletal muscles – and exercising our large muscle groups is important for a long list of reasons. Exercise improves bone strength and posture, helps us balance our energy intake, enhances mood and cognitive function, and improves heart and lung function, just to name a few benefits.

As we saw earlier, exercise builds muscle, and it's the amount of muscle we carry that has the most profound effect on our metabolic rate, and therefore our ability to burn the calories we ingest. I'm going to get a bit science-y here but bear with me, because it may just convince you to see exercise as your number-one ally in long-term weight management.

Okay, the body is made up of around 40 trillion cells (and remember that 1 trillion is a million times a million). Inside each cell are tiny little dudes called mitochondria, whose main job is to oxidise ('burn') carbohydrates, amino acids and fatty acids to make adenosine triphosphate (ATP) – the energy our cells need to perform their functions. Basically, without ATP, there is no life.

Mitochondria are in the cells of every organ and tissue in the human body: the brain, heart, lungs, liver, muscles and tendons (red blood cells are the only ones without them). In our muscle cells there are hundreds or even thousands of mitochondria to help them generate the large quantities of ATP needed during exercise. Plus, when we exercise, mitochondria replicate themselves ('mitochondrial biogenesis'), increasing the muscle's ability to take up glucose during and after exercise. This is why our muscles are so important in helping us to burn calories and balance our energy intake.

> At fifty-one, I still love exercising hard daily and seriously put the young girls to shame at the gym.
>
> Therese

Exercise also reduces anxiety and improves mood, meaning we're less likely to crave alcohol or carbs to deal with stress. In fact, many studies have concluded that regular exercise (whether cardio or weight training or both) is as effective as medication in treating depressive disorder. But even if you're not someone who feels anxious or depressed, exercise is freaking awesome because it makes you feel good. Exercising makes us happy. And when something makes us feel good right now, we're more likely to do it – more so than if we are doing it for some benefit way off in the future (such as fitting into a dress or living longer).

Weight loss aside, there is also increasing evidence that overweight individuals who are physically active can significantly reduce their risks of cardiovascular disease and diabetes. Indeed, studies show that people who are overweight but fit have lower risks of carking it than non-exercising people whose weight is average for their height.

Training has always been my rock. Even sometimes when I don't want to do it, it's like an old friend who just says, 'Come on, get your runners on, girlfriend! You'll be fine!' and even if I get off to a bumpy start, I always feel better when I'm done. In fact, when things are literally going bonkers in my life, that's when I know I need to train. It grounds me, it centres me and it allows me to switch off. Exercising my body gives me a greater perspective on life and what's really important.

So, if you're a jogger, a bike rider, a sport player or just a fast walker – keep it up and more power to you. The more you move each day, the more muscle mass you build and the better your chances of keeping excess kilos at bay and disease away.

If you're new to daily exercise, have a look at some of the gear-free workouts I've suggested on page 282. Oh, and amp up your incidental exercise. It's pretty easy:

- Take the goddamned stairs!
- Walk to work or to meetings or to the shops.
- If you sit at a desk for a job, set your alarm and get up every 20 minutes and MOVE.

Mish says...

Mark has his routine down pat, so for him there's no longer a need to consistently be drawing on willpower, or having to always talk himself into a workout and out of the chocolate cake. It's just a way of life.

CASE STUDY

I have gone from 103 to 87 kg and kept it off for over nine years now. Used to be crippled every couple of weeks with sciatica and had two knee arthroscopes nine years ago. Now I am a gym junkie and have zero health issues, so well worth the hard work. Still have to keep it in check and weigh myself daily and keep an eye on the calories. — MARK

NICOLE'S STORY

My story is like many others. I always struggled with weight (I can remember being eight and thinking my sister was so much thinner than I was). This was exacerbated by poor decisions in my adolescent years, which then led to my twenties – it was then that I reconnected with exercise. I joined a gym at work and worked out before work, at lunchtime or after work and lost 20 kg. At the time I thought I needed to lose another 10, but photos tell a very different story. I looked awesome. If I could be as 'overweight' as I was in my wedding photos I would be frickin' delighted!

I then had a baby, carried the weight for about two years, shifted it, got pregnant, had a second child and again carried the weight for about two years before losing it again.

After my third (and final) child I put on more weight and was sitting at about 95 kg. I went to an opera night, in 2012 I think. The next day I was in bed looking at the photos, hating what I was seeing. I signed up for my first round of 12WBT. I was committed. It didn't feel like a sacrifice – it felt like I was part of a team. The results were amazing and kept coming. I can't actually remember how many rounds I did, but I ended up at about 72 kg.

The next couple of years I kept the weight off, ran a marathon and generally felt awesome, but somehow the good eating went by the wayside. I am completely committed to my exercise (I now need it for my mental health as much as anything!), but the decisions surrounding what I eat and drink seem to sit in a different part of my brain. This part is much more flexible and easily influenced, by children, stress, heat, boyfriends, ex-husbands, finances – the list is endless. The excuses are inexhaustible. I would not dream of not working out before my day begins, but what I fuel myself with can change on a whim (even as I type this I am thinking, 'Who is this fruit cake with the split personality??'). I am currently sitting at 84 kg and hating it. I do at least thirty minutes' exercise six days a week, from HIIT to a jog, kettle bells, TRX, pilates, yoga – you name it, I'll try it.

The other part of this strange self-sabotaging struggle (that is fabulous alliteration – you may use this :)) is that I actually love cooking and making good food. I love going to the markets and buying fresh produce, planning recipes that I can prepare ahead of time and freeze for my lunches, etc. When I look at it, I fear I still use alcohol and food as a 'reward'.

I need to lose 10 kg, reclaim my wardrobe and kick some more fitness goals. I appreciate all that you and your fabulous team have done, Mish, to help all of us be our best selves, and will continue to read and follow your amazing inroads to changing Australia's (and the rest of the world's) relationship with our bodies and realising our full potential.

Mish says...

Nicole's story tells us she has her environment well and truly set up for her exercise, and her WHY around her training is strong and real. It's for her. Her food choices are also set in a routine; however it's one that is setting her back. Swapping out old habits with new ones, like going for a run before reaching for a glass of wine, can work, but there needs to be some thoughtful introspection around how to handle stress and why it triggers poor choices. Clearing out the house of junk food or alcohol is one thing, but clearing out the thoughts of 'I need/ deserve/can't live without that piece of cake' takes a bit more work. Work worth doing though!

3 GET SUPPORT

There is a lot of research to show that social networks are powerful tools in encouraging positive health behaviour. This is one of the reasons I loved setting up my 12WBT program, as it supports people while they take steps to improve their mindset, nutrition and exercise habits. But if the 'it takes a village' mentality seems too crowded for your liking, having a support crew in the single digits can often be just as effective. Getting your best friend or your two workout buddies or your significant other plus your kids in your corner to cheer you on and keep you consistent can work wonders. The key is to keep it going – make time to check in and update your cheer squad on how you're travelling. They can cheer you up when things are tough, and cheer you on when you're firing on all cylinders!

> *Mish says...*
>
> Support is not critical but very, very powerful. Having a workout buddy or a support network can be extremely rewarding, and fun!

CASE · STUDY

About five years ago I hit 100 kg. I was so embarrassed and disgusted by myself and I didn't want to feel that way any longer. Not long after that I met my now-husband and we decided to go on this crazy journey together! It has been a very slow learning process and I didn't set a goal weight until about a year before our wedding. I reached this goal a month before our wedding and lost a total of 30 kg. My husband also reached his goal and lost 40 kg! — JESSIE

INVITE YOUR FAMILY ON BOARD

One of the most common reasons people give for not being able to maintain a healthy weight is that their family is not on board. I hear things like, 'My husband hates salad', 'My kids won't eat veggies', 'I haven't got time to make three different meals', etc. And yes, I get how challenging it can be when your family is not supportive, but it is vital to at least try to have a proper 'enrolment conversation' with them. This means a screen-free family meeting where you explain the changes you want to make to the food you share as a family and why it is so important, not only for your own physical and mental health, but also the health of everyone else. You need to blow them away with your honesty and courage, which will happen naturally if you speak from the heart.

If they are resistant, you may need to take it slowly, and choose your battles. If you are in charge of shopping and cooking, and your partner and children have never shown any interest in helping you, then you obviously have more of a say. (Sometimes I need to give my clients a gentle nudge to remind them they are the grown-up, the leader, the BOSS!) It may be rocky at times, but remember these positive changes benefit everyone and will set your kids on the path to a longer, healthier life.

HANG OUT WITH LIKE-MINDED BUDDIES

Having an exercise partner can be a powerful motivator to get you out of bed in the mornings to go walking or jogging. Joining an exercise class is great, too, as most of us don't like to waste money so we're more likely to turn up. You can also join sporting clubs, walking groups, cycling groups or even take dancing classes – you're only limited by your imagination. Whatever you do, surround yourself with people who also care about their own health and wellbeing, as research has shown that having an overweight or obese best friend significantly reduces your chances of maintaining a healthy weight. In a small 2008 Melbourne study, for example, researchers found that obese people who successfully lost weight experienced a lot of pressure from friends and family to regain the weight – 'You look sick', 'You look too thin', 'Being thin doesn't suit you', etc – and deliberately placed them in situations to test their resistance to crap food. While this sabotage may have been unconscious, it still places enormous pressure on people who lose weight: 'They won't love me if I'm thinner.'

Sometimes when we make a change in our lives, it challenges the stories people have about how we fit into their world. Friends, family or colleagues may push back (consciously or unconsciously) because it works better to have you as you were. If you were the 'fat friend' or the 'booze buddy' or the 'Maccas mate' and now you're not, who then is going to fulfil that role so they can keep playing theirs? Rather than finding a new person to write that storyline with, they try to get you to go back to your old ways.

It can be hard, but it's important to have an honest conversation about your goals, and to give those friends a chance to support the new you. And if they don't want to, that's okay. While it may be hurtful, it's their choice, just as it's your choice to live a healthy life. There's nothing wrong with letting go of relationships that don't work for you. Those friends that do embrace your new way of being are the lifetime friends and you want to put your energy into continuing to nurture those relationships.

BE KIND TO YOURSELF

In recent years, there has been a lot of research about the stigma associated with obesity and how it contributes to sufferers' poor self-esteem, high rates of depression and reluctance to seek help. As I explained in Part One, people living with obesity are often labelled as lazy and unmotivated, and yet many are doing the best they can given the powerful physiological and environmental factors at play.

Working in the fitness industry I see first-hand how important it is for people to have faith in themselves, because without it, reaching a healthy weight is an uphill battle. Indeed, research shows that people with poor body image (whether they are just overweight or morbidly obese) will find it much harder to lose weight, let alone keep it off. In my book *Your Best Body* I talked about the comparison trap, and how destructive it is to compare ourselves to others and to the unrealistic images of the so-called 'beautiful' people in the public eye (who have often had a hair and makeup team working on them for hours and are photoshopped to within an inch of their lives).

Accepting our bodies – no matter what shape or weight we are – is the first step to looking after ourselves. I know this sounds disingenuous when I run a business that talks about 'transforming' your body, but without this grounding self-acceptance, any changes you make are always going to be forced – more like punishment than nourishment. So please be gentle with yourself. You are so much more than a number on a set of scales. When you buy fresh veggies, or cook a healthy meal, or go for a long walk, tell yourself how amazing you are. Don't wait for someone else to do it!

Mish says...

We all have days when, for whatever reason, we don't eat well or we miss a workout. I enjoy a glass of wine now and then. It's called being human. I love that Kathryn and Sue have recognised that this doesn't mean we wave the white flag and chuck it all in. Our habits and routines are still there. We pick up and move on.

I still enjoy a glass of wine and an occasional takeaway but I don't beat myself up over that – I know now I have the tools to put it right again.

Sue

CASE STUDY

I struggle with emotional eating like most people. But I realise that if I have a bad meal or even a bad day I just pick up the pieces and jump back on that wagon. I love all the energy I have now. I can keep up with my ten year old and I'll never look back. I have the willpower now to say no to certain foods and even certain situations that I know are no good for me. I have more confidence and am happier in myself. I have done four of your [12WBT] rounds and now use your recipes to make my own meal plans. — KATHRYN

SEEK HELP FOR EMOTIONAL PROBLEMS

Sometimes, though, no matter how hard we try, some of us will continue to rely on food or alcohol to comfort us and we will overindulge to the point that it affects our daily life. Remember there's a difference between habits and addictions. Habits we can work on ourselves, while the deeper emotional and mental health issues that can lead to addictions often require specialist intervention. There's no shame in seeking professional help from a doctor or therapist if you are struggling – in fact, it's the straight-up sensible thing to do.

4 ALWAYS CHOOSE FRESH WHOLEFOODS

One mistake many people make when they reach their goal weight is to treat themselves to unhealthy foods. I've seen this happen again and again. They think that because they've lost a lot of weight, it won't hurt to eat the odd sugary, fatty meal. But a burger here, a slice of cheesecake with cream there, and soon they're back to the same old eating patterns that saw them gain so much weight in the first place. From personal experience, choosing healthy food *every single day* is non-negotiable when it comes to long-term weight management. The research shows that people who do keep the weight off stick to a diet that is high in fibre and nutrients from vegetables, fruits, legumes and wholegrains and with a good amount of healthy fats from olive oil, nuts and seeds. (And remember one of my favourite sayings: veggies are the rockstars, meat is the backup singer!)

A 2011 longitudinal study of weight gain in 120,000 men and women in the US found that people on average gain half a kilo a year, and that the people who gained the most weight ate more French fries, potato chips, potatoes, sugar-sweetened drinks, red meat and processed meats (no surprises there!). And the *least* weight gain was associated with the consumption of yoghurt, nuts, fruits, wholegrains and vegetables, in that order. So, if you feel you'd like a treat, make it good-quality plain yoghurt with some fresh berries (or my Raspberry Cheesecake Fingers on page 147).

If you've already lost a fair bit of weight, you'll know all about how to set yourself up for success. If you're at the start of your weight-loss journey then the info on the next few pages – about how to set up a sensible pantry and practical tips on meal prep – will get you on the right track. Plus there's plenty more ideas in Part Three.

Learning about foods and the taste of natural unprocessed foods has been like clearing out the clutter in my head.

Molly

STAPLES

PANTRY STAPLES

- capers
- coconut cream
- light coconut milk
- miso paste
- mirin
- mustard: dijon; wholegrain
- nori (seaweed) sheets
- tahini (unhulled)
- tamari (gluten-free soy sauce)
- tinned red salmon
- tinned tuna in springwater
- tomato passata; tomato paste
- vinegar: apple cider; balsamic; red wine; white wine

OILS

- avocado oil
- coconut oil and cooking spray
- extra virgin olive oil and cooking spray
- extra light olive oil
- macadamia oil
- sesame oil

GRAINS, LENTILS & BEANS

- bread: mountain bread; rye; sourdough
- couscous (wholemeal)
- noodles: brown rice vermicelli; soba
- oats: quick; rolled
- pasta (wholemeal)
- polenta
- rice: brown basmati; puffed; wild
- lentils: brown; dried split red
- beans: black; butter; cannellini; red kidney
- chickpeas

NUTS, SEEDS & DRIED FRUIT

- almonds: whole; flaked; slivered; almond meal; almond spread
- brazil nuts
- cashews
- coconut: flaked; shredded; desiccated; coconut flour
- hazelnuts
- macadamias
- pecans
- pine nuts
- pistachios
- walnuts
- chia seeds
- linseeds
- pumpkin seeds
- sesame seeds
- sunflower seeds
- quinoa: flakes; puffed; seeds
- craisins (dried cranberries)
- freeze-dried strawberries

HERBS & SPICES

- sea salt
- pepper: cracked black; ground white
- dried mixed herbs
- allspice
- cajun seasoning
- cayenne pepper
- cinnamon: ground; sticks
- coriander: ground; seeds
- cumin: ground; seeds
- curry powder
- chilli: flakes; powder
- dukkah
- fennel seeds
- mixed spice
- mustard seeds
- nutmeg
- oregano
- paprika
- saffron
- sumac
- tarragon
- turmeric

BAKING & SWEET TREATS

- baking powder
- bicarbonate of soda
- dark chocolate (70–80 per cent cocoa)
- flours: arrowroot (tapioca flour); cornflour; rice flour; self-raising wholemeal; plain wholemeal
- honey
- pure maple syrup
- raw cacao powder
- unsweetened apple puree
- vanilla bean paste or extract

FRIDGE STAPLES

- butter
- cheese: cheddar (tasty); cottage; Danish feta; mozzarella; parmesan; ricotta
- eggs
- fermented slaw
- labne
- milk: unsweetened almond milk; rice milk
- olives: green; kalamata
- stock: chicken; vegetable
- tofu: firm
- yoghurt: full-cream Greek

FREEZER STAPLES

- blueberries; mixed berries; raspberries
- baby peas
- edamame (soybeans)

I have what I call emergency meals in the freezer
for when I get home late and cannot be bothered cooking.

Katie

SHOPPING TIPS

→ Always take a list: keep a list on the fridge or in your phone so that you can add to it as you run out of staples

→ Buy the foods you need for the coming week plus a little extra for freezing

→ Never shop hungry: always have a full tummy when you're food shopping to avoid being tempted by dumb food choices

→ Take a water bottle and sip on it: this will help you steer yourself towards the fruit and veggies and away from the packet crap

→ If possible, buy your fruit and veggies from a grocer, farmers' market or even online

→ When you're at the supermarket, get your staples and get out: remember, the real foods tend to be found around the edges of the supermarket, so start there and stay there. Keep away from the aisles of precooked, heavily processed foods, confectionery and chips, and avert your eyes at the checkout!

MEAL PREP TIPS

Sometimes life gets *really busy*. You know the deal – you're working part-time and you have to take three kids to different sport/music/whatever practice venues and then get home and cook dinner. This is why it is *so* important to plan ahead.

On Sundays, always look at your week ahead and plan your meals so that on those crazy busy nights you will have some leftovers or a previously prepared and frozen meal that you can get on the table quick sticks. That way, you're less likely to be caught short and find yourself tempted by takeaway rubbish.

YOUR FREEZER IS YOUR FRIEND

Let's face it. Cooking up double batches and freezing the extra is how most busy parents survive. Who has got the time to source separate ingredients for twenty-one meals a week! So, I always make sure I include recipes with freezer-friendly ingredients (and in this book, I've included a whole chapter on batch cooking and freezing; see page 231).

WHEN IN DOUBT, BARBECUE

I love my barbecue. Honestly, it is probably my number-one cooking appliance. It's just so easy to slice up some zucchini, pumpkin and broccolini, brush them with a little olive oil and chargrill them alongside some fresh fish or chicken tenders. I guess it's something about cooking outside that just feels right. (Of course, I don't stand out there when it's wintry and cold – that's when I love to roast veggies in the oven and make big batches of soup.)

LOVING YOUR LEFTOVERS

There's no rule book that says you have to cook a different meal every night – I mean who came up with that one? If it suits you to cook up a big chicken dish one night and then have it again a couple of nights later, why not? It's not only time-saving for you but also energy-saving for the planet. I always try to include recipes that are delicious the next day. I also love using part of a meal to create a new one – say, shredding some leftover barbecued meat and tossing it through a fresh salad. See pages 249–267 for plenty of ideas to create delicious meals with leftovers.

ORDER AHEAD ONLINE

Having a regular standard shopping delivery (either for groceries or fruit and veg, or both) can often save time and headspace. You always know you have the basics there to create a fast meal. Often if it's a seasonal box of produce, it can inspire me to use ingredients I may not have used for ages, and be a little creative.

Food prepping is a must. Even if you eat the same lunch every day for a week it's worth it.

Renee

EAT MINDFULLY

So much of the eating we do is automatic. We do it in front of the TV or while we're walking to catch a bus, or even while we're shopping – shovelling food in without even really registering what it is.

Mindful eating is about slowing things right down: paying attention to our own hunger signals; enjoying food in a quiet, screen-free environment; noticing the colour, texture and flavour of the food; chewing slowly and putting down our utensils between mouthfuls. Deliberately slowing down your eating can help you feel fuller and it definitely assists digestion. But mindfulness is also important when we're deciding what and when to eat.

EAT THREE MEALS, STARTING WITH BREAKFAST

I know I've said this in all of my books, but it is so important that it's worth repeating:

You.

Must.

Eat.

Breakfast.

(Preferably with some protein.)

In my experience, skipping breakfast is the number-one habit shared by all of my obese clients, closely followed at number two by lack of exercise. Enjoying a good breakfast with wholegrain carbs, greens such as spinach and proteins such as eggs or beans will kick-start your metabolism and keep you feeling full until lunchtime. If you skip breakfast, your brain doesn't get the fresh hit of glucose it needs to operate at full throttle, so it releases appetite hormones that signal you need high-sugar foods and you need them now! Which is why so many breakfast-skippers are hoeing into a sugary muffin as big as their head by 10.30 am.

Even if you're not particularly hungry in the morning (which, I might add, means you probably ate too much the night before), eat *something*. Give your body the much-needed fuel it requires to power you through the first part of your day.

KATE'S STORY

What made you decide to lose weight in the first place? What was your WHY?

I noticed that I'd put on a bit of weight and really wanted to get it down to avoid the weight struggles getting to be overwhelming as I got older.

Did you set a goal weight?

Yes, and I ended up FAR exceeding that. I started at 72 kg, set my goal weight for 68 kg. I got down to 61.5 kg by the end of round one!!

How much weight in total did you lose?

I lost 10 kg in total!

How long were you able to maintain this goal weight?

I set my goal weight too modestly. I lost 7 kg more than my goal. I've been able to keep my weight down for four years now! I maintain a training regime and have all the tools to modify and review my diet when I notice any weight creeping back on.

What are the key factors that you think either helped or hindered your ability to manage your weight?

- Reviewing my portions and my diet habits was vital. Recognising how I eat, when I eat and what I eat. Having a new understanding of how much is necessary to eat, rather than eating what I wanted.

- Definitely Michelle's videos. Her key messages were always spot-on with where my head was at. Four years on, I still feel I have Michelle in my head with her messages.

- Having a routine for exercises, and guidance on what to do. I still plan my weekly exercise today, four years on. It eliminates the decision/dilemma in my head, as I have a plan and then I stick to it!

- Menu planning was huge!!! Having a plan was really helpful, and something I do still today.

- I commenced 12WBT with a friend. Doing this with a local friend was huge for me. I didn't need the online support, as I had a real-life friend to share it with!

I've discovered a whole new world in training/exercise and achieved more than I ever imagined my body would cope with. I just wish I'd discovered this twenty years earlier! But I'm super proud to now be forty and fitter and stronger than I have ever been, or would ever have dreamt of being! Thanks Michelle! Many, many, many friends have done your program since, having seen the dramatic 360 my life took with weight loss and exercise as a focus, so I consider that my gift. xxx

---

Mish says...

Kate has her routine and habits set. Four years of the same mindful choices, regular and consistent. This routine takes the daily deliberation (which is exhausting) out of the picture, freeing us up to JFDI!

KEEP AN EYE ON YOUR SERVING SIZES

As we saw in Part One, many people who lose weight can experience the physiological double-whammy: a slowed metabolism (particularly when they don't do enough exercise) and heightened appetite. And if you happen to be under a fair amount of stress and aren't sleeping well, it can be challenging to keep your serving sizes under control, as you may feel more vulnerable and this could knock out routines that aren't well entrenched. Yet portion control is key to maintaining your weight. This is why I've always provided calorie counts in my recipes, as it gives you a visual understanding of the correct serving sizes.

Having said that, I should explain that, personally, I don't need to count calories nor do many people I've worked with, because we've got ourselves to a place where we know what our portions should look like and we simply stick to them. We are like well-oiled machines; it's just become a habit.

Every client I've ever worked with has asked, 'Please tell me what to eat', which is why I always provide low-calorie, high-nutrient recipes that I know will keep you inspired in the kitchen, and provide the energy you need for optimum health. The 'maintenance' recipes in this book are designed to provide 1500 calories per day for women (three main meals @ 400 calories, plus two snacks @ 150). For men, children and growing teenagers (or for those days where you need more fuel due to harder workouts), I also provide 'boosts' of 50/100/150/200 calories. However, as we have seen, our bodies have some powerful physiological responses to dieting, so if you notice your weight creeping up, either remove your snacks for a while, or use the 'reset' recipes (three main meals @ 300 calories, plus two snacks @ 150 calories).

If you follow my recipes you will automatically control your serving sizes, but here are some general tips:

- Never go back for seconds.
- Avoid foods in a box or bag – serve some on a plate and put the rest away.
- Don't eat in front of the TV, computer or at your desk at work. When you are distracted, it's harder to pay attention to what you are eating.
- Drink plenty of water throughout the day. Sometimes we think we're hungry when we're actually thirsty, so if you think you're hungry, have a glass of water first.

Portion
control is key
to maintaining
your weight.

54

TAKE CONTROL WHEN EATING OUT

Many clients and quite a few of my 12WBTers have told me how difficult it is to manage their weight over Christmas or when they go on holidays, and that these were the times they tended to slip back into old habits. Now just because you're managing your weight doesn't mean that you have to become a social outcast, or that you have to take your calorie counter with you whenever you're eating out with friends. I *love* going out for a meal. And not just dinner either. There's nothing better than a Saturday brekkie or a Sunday lunch. The good news is that with a little knowledge and some smart food choices, eating out can be thoroughly enjoyable *and* healthy.

The important thing to remember is that chefs want their food to plug into our reward pathways so that we keep coming back, which means adding lots of salt, fats and sugar. If you eat out *a lot* you will not only struggle to lose weight, but also keep it off. So, choose carefully and be prepared to ask the serving staff a few questions.

Here are a few of my rules when eating out:

- Don't go out in starvation mode. If dinner or lunch is later than usual, have a boiled egg, or half a banana with a few nuts, or some carrot sticks and hummus.
- Share a main with someone else and have it with a side of salad or veggies.
- If it's a banquet, serve yourself the meat and vegetables and steer clear of the rice, bread and anything crumbed and stuffed.
- Choose barbecued, grilled or steamed over fried or oven-roasted.
- Ask for any sauces or dressings to be served on the side so that you can control how much oil, salt and sugar you're adding to your food.
- Avoid alcohol, as for some, it's a trigger to let go. Not only is it empty calories, but it weakens your resolve. Offer to be the driver and go for sparkling mineral water with sliced lemon or lime.
- Simply smile at people who tease you about your food choices. You don't need to explain anything. What you eat is *not* their business. This comes back to the 'hang out with like-minded buddies' point I mentioned earlier. If your friends are giving you grief, chances are they are trying to get you to behave like the 'old you' who fits in with their story. Once you understand it from that perspective, it can be easier to take the emotion out of it and just not engage. Let them tease. It'll soon get boring when you don't respond.
- Eat slowly. Remember, you don't have to lick the plate clean! If you are satisfied, put your cutlery together on the plate along with your serviette. This sends a clear signal that you are finished.

6 KEEP TRACK

I know this might sound a bit obvious, but we can only change behaviours that we're aware of. Keeping track of what we eat, how much we exercise and our weight helps us to understand the relationship between these behaviours and reinforces positive change. In fact, the research clearly shows that people who monitor their food intake and regularly weigh themselves are far more likely to maintain a healthy weight over the long term.

This is the main reason I encourage people to understand calories, as it helps them to pay attention to what they are eating. Naysayers tell me that focusing on calories not only ignores the reality that different foods have different effects on metabolism, but also creates an obsessive relationship with food. And yes, I agree that not all calories are equal, but I have always advocated avoiding alcohol, sugar, refined grains and unhealthy fats, and instead getting your energy from wholegrains, vegetables and lean protein. (No one who reads my books is going to serve themselves a bowl of Fruit Loops and say, 'Well that's my 400 calories for breakfast!'.) Also, as I explained earlier, counting calories isn't something you have to do for every single meal for the rest of your life. Once you get an idea of the energy values of different foods, you'll be able to get your portions right without the calculations. If you find that your weight does start to creep up, it's easy to do a week of calorie counting to get your eye back in. There are a bunch of calorie counting and workout tracking apps that you can download to your phone or computer, and a lot of the great ones are free.

If you are an emotional eater, it can also be great to keep track of your moods, and how they relate to the foods and/or physical activity you're doing. If you enjoy writing, keeping a journal can be a wonderful way to keep track of your progress. Or you can keep a digital record on your phone or computer (the 'My Tracker' feature in 12WBT tracks mood, sleep, water and food intake, and workouts).

And even if you have days or weeks where you don't do as well, don't despair. Think of these times as reality checks, as opportunities to press the reset button, and be grateful that you're smart enough and brave enough to take good care of yourself.

> Now I am eating more wholefoods, a good amount of protein,
> good fats, no grains or pasta and very little sugar. I feel full
> and never hungry, which feels much more sustainable.
> It really is a journey, isn't it?
>
> Meaghan

SHARON'S STORY

What made you decide to lose weight in the first place? What was your WHY?

I was fast heading towards fifty and decided it was time to do something for me! I wanted to be fit, healthy and lose some weight – 12WBT gave me all the tools to do this.

Did you set a goal weight?

Yes – I was 84 kg and wanted to get to 72 kg as I felt this was a weight I could maintain.

Did you reach your goal weight?

Yes – I lost exactly 12 kg in the first round. Then I wanted to maintain this weight but increase the exercise so I signed up for another round and lost another 2 kg.

How much weight in total did you lose?

14 kg.

How long were you able to maintain this goal weight?

At the end of my second round I had lost a total of 14 kg. I now fluctuate between the 70 kg–72 kg mark. I have just had two weeks' holidays and have gone up to 73 kg so to keep on track I have pulled out a weekly meal plan and will follow it for a few weeks to make sure I keep on track. I still exercise five times a week and love it – with kids' sport on Saturdays I have found it hard to do the Super Saturday sessions over summer, though I loved the sense of achievement after finishing them and will reintroduce them when 'winter sport' moves to a Sunday. The exercise program on the 12WBT program is fantastic – it has heaps of variety, which keeps it interesting especially when exercising to the Michelle Bridges soundtracks!!

What are the key factors that you think either helped or hindered your ability to manage your weight?

My inspiration at the beginning was proving the 'negative people' who said I wouldn't stick to it wrong. Once I started seeing results and receiving compliments for the change, it spurred me on but the biggest thing to help me keep going is that I feel so much better. When I am in the gym it always amazes me when I am doing step-ups holding 14 kg of weights that I used to carry that 14 kg around every day!

Mish says...

Sharon's story talks about consistency. Forward planning. Accountability. Checking in and being mindful. Again, habits and routines. Sharon has worked her routine around her life, tweaked it and made it her own and chooses to see it through the eyes of how it makes her feel. It's a gift! Not a chore.

7 MAKE SLEEP A PRIORITY

I have placed this tip last, but it is by no means the least important. As I explained in Part One, lack of sleep increases your appetite for sweet food, as your brain thinks it's going to need more fuel to cope with the extra hours you're awake. Being sleep deprived also makes you more sensitive to stress which can trigger the stress hormones that encourage belly fat.

But weight management is only a tiny part of the importance of sleep. When we rest, our bodies do all the amazing repair jobs that need to be done to keep us firing on all cylinders. If we don't get enough sleep we can't concentrate, our short-term memory is affected and we're physically clumsy and have poor reaction times. We also risk falling asleep at the wheel when we're driving – need I say more?

Are you the kind of person who sits up late at night watching TV or on Facebook? Have you ever wondered how this is serving you? One of the most common traits in my clients who were wanting to lose weight was that they were night owls. Not only does the lack of sleep have a physiological impact as explained above, but you are more likely to snack at this time, and a late night can leave you not wanting to get up early the next day to work out. A triple whammy!

To give yourself the best chance of staying on track with healthy eating (and not falling in a heap when it comes time to exercise), it is super important to get seven–eight hours of sleep every night. You'll find that your mind is much clearer, your willpower is stronger and that you can stay on-task.

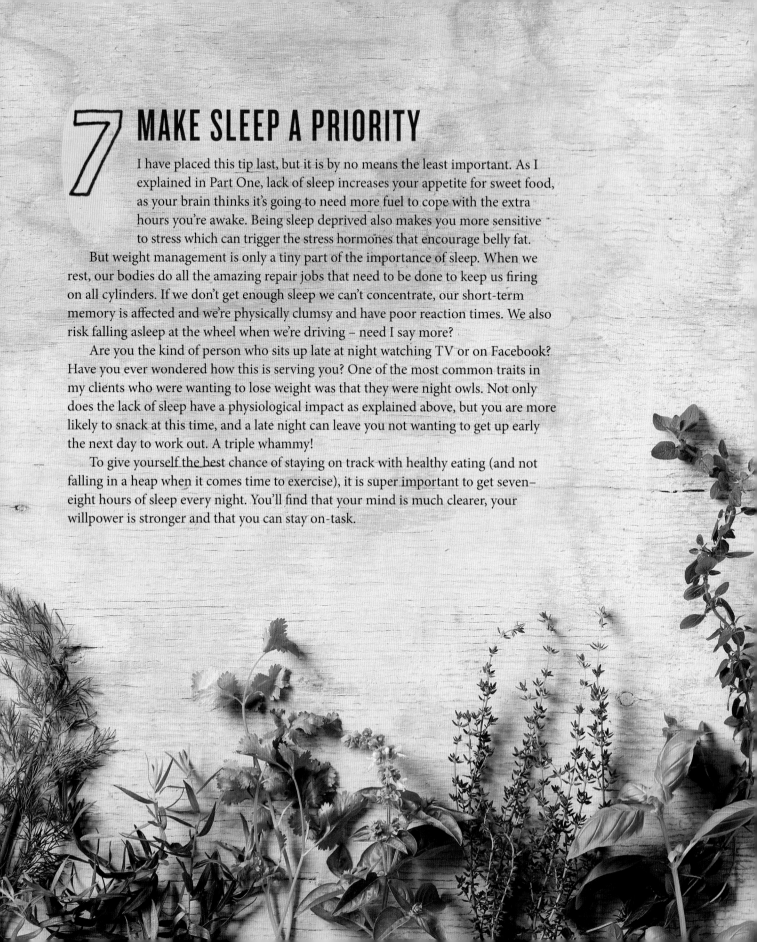

TIPS FOR GETTING A GOOD NIGHT'S SLEEP

→ **Go to bed a bit earlier.** Even half an hour earlier will help.

→ **Avoid backlit screens at bedtime.** When there is less light at the end of the day, our body clock (a bunch of cells in the hypothalamus) triggers the production of melatonin, the hormone that makes us feel drowsy and helps us fall asleep. Obviously, working on screens is not going to help your brain register that it's sleep time, so put 'em away for at least half an hour before bed.

→ **Keep your bedroom dark.** Like backlit screens, having light seeping in through thin curtains, or LED lights glowing on your digital alarm clock, can interrupt the production of melatonin and deprive you of a decent night's sleep. Get block-out curtains or blinds, swap your electric digital alarm clock for an old-school analogue and reap the sleepy-time rewards!

→ **Have a winding-down ritual.** Studies show that the brain learns to switch into rest mode if you perform the same little rituals every night. It might be as simple as cleaning your teeth then reading a book, or having a chamomile tea and doing a restful yoga pose – whatever works for you.

→ **Make a to-do list.** People who worry a lot can find it hard to fall asleep. If you are a worrier, it can be helpful to make a short list of things you want to do the next day. Our brains are problem-solving machines, so just the act of writing a list is a 'solution', allowing us to relax and go to sleep.

→ **Avoid stimulants in the evening.** This includes coffee, chocolate, tea (even green tea), chillies or other spicy foods. Caffeine has a long half-life – meaning it stays in your system for a long time. If you are someone who feels anxious or stressed a lot, it can be helpful to limit your caffeine intake to the morning only.

→ **Get up at the same time each day** and give your eyes a good dose of natural light (either go outside, or look out a window). I know this sounds odd, but it really does help to reset your body clock, and to make you more alert.

A DAY IN THE LIFE...

I have a crazy schedule, different from one day to the next, so I have to build as much routine in as I can to keep the wheels turning. This means that planning is critical, so I know where I'm heading that day, how I'm getting there, when I'll be home, will we need a babysitter, and where can I fit my workout in? It's *all* about forward planning.

But just because I have an unorthodox schedule, I'm not going to stop taking care of myself. Just like you, I need to keep up with my training, keep eating well and keep my head in check. I don't get a free ride or have a 'lucky' gene pool. It's a daily renewable contract for me just as it is for you. Rather than fight it or give up, I accept it and work around it. That's my reframe.

I have no set time for training, although I do try to get it done in the morning if possible, before life gets complicated. If I have to be on set, though, the hair and makeup team arrive at my home around 5.45am, so on those days, I'll train in the afternoon or in the evening. And, if I finish really late and miss training, I'll make sure I eat really light that day to keep things in check. My training is usually a mix of strength and mixed strength/cardio circuits. Some days are tougher than others, and sometimes I dial it right back and feel extremely happy that I simply kept the routine.

I usually wake at 6am with Axel and we all eat breakfast together (normally eggs on sourdough with avo and spinach). Or if we are needing more greens because we've been travelling or just feel like a pump-up, we'll do a green smoothie. If I'm going to be out all day, I'll throw together a packed lunch (usually a tuna salad or a chicken salad sandwich) and then take a moment to think about dinner. Who's home tonight? Do I need to pull something out of the freezer? Is there anything I can prep now that will make life a little bit easier tonight? This is one of our secrets of success – we always try to discuss dinner at breakfast. Sounds bonkers, but it's a great tip.

> Just like you, I need to keep up with my training,
> keep eating well and keep my head in check.

If I'm home for lunch, I'll make myself a salad or have leftovers from dinner the night before. If I'm on set, it's usually a buffet-style lunch, which can be dangerous! My strategy is to choose a small plate of what I know is good for me, and then excuse myself and make a phone call or check my emails straight after I've eaten so I don't go back for seconds. Within 10 minutes, I feel full and I'm good.

Whether I'm travelling, on a shoot or working from home, I try to incorporate lots of movement into my day. I take the stairs at the airport, I get up from my desk at home every 30 minutes and move, and if I'm on set, I'll help move the set around or pick up equipment to help out. Why not!? We are designed to move, so I seek out every opportunity to do so.

Now, I don't know about you, but I reckon snacks have been taken to a whole new height of overdone. More often than not I think it's boredom or sheer force of habit that has us reaching for a mid-morning or mid-afternoon snack. My tip? Check in with your stomach. If it's growling, have an apple. If not, get on with your day.

When dinnertime rolls around, if I'm away from home and staying in a hotel, I'll order steamed veggies and fish or chicken for dinner. If I'm at home, it's a matter of heating up the food I grabbed from the freezer that morning and adding some freshly steamed greens, or maybe throwing some chicken breasts or beef fillet on the barbie to serve with some pre-prepped veg.

Some days, though, the system fails, and there's been many an arvo when Steve and I have texted each other with 'What are we doing for dinner?' 'Dunno. What do you feel like?' 'Dunno. What's in the fridge?' 'Nothing.' And I feel like a complete failure! On days like this, we always have a few key staples in our pantry to fall back on. A couple of tins of tuna, some rice or quinoa, then I'll pick up some lettuce, cucumber, feta and tomatoes on the way home, and boom!

And of course, if the day has been a total ball-slammer, then I'll have a light dinner and do my training at 8:30pm. It's not my favourite time to train, and if I'm honest I'd rather sit on the couch and watch TV, but it clears my head and I always feel so good afterwards.

Ultimately, all I can offer you is my experience, which may give rise to a new way of thinking for you. When I consider those people I know who consistently maintain good health and fitness, there are some common behaviours. They have solid routines in place, which in turn create good habits, and these tend to quash any internal negotiating or overthinking. This frees them up and allows them space to give more energy to other areas of their life. For them, eating healthily and getting regular exercise is as routine as brushing their teeth or making the bed. It's just part of the everyday normal – no fanfare or emotional turmoil, they just get on with it. There's also a sense that they choose to do these things, as opposed to thinking they have to. That alone is a very powerful 'reframe'.

I'm gonna put a concept forward. I reckon it's the internal battle that's exhausting. Consider this. Could the constant internal and external negotiating be more draining than doing 30 minutes of exercise? Could the endless deliberating, negative self-talk, feelings of missing out and beat-ups exhaust you more than being organised? It's at least worth considering.

Like anything new, taking on new ideas means you start as a beginner. That's another 'reframe' right there. Giving yourself permission to be a beginner. With patience and love. After all, it's a long life and we are all still learning.

PART THREE

PLANS, PORTIONS & PROTOCOLS

The following pages contain tons of great tips on how to get organised in the kitchen. These really are your secret weapon to consistent, sustainable healthy eating – the idea is that with a little thought and pre-planning, even the most time-poor, flat-strapped of us can enjoy nutritious, home-cooked food each and every day.

MEAL PLANS

On the following pages are six different meal plans to choose from, with accompanying shopping lists. I want to reiterate that I don't personally count calories, and I'm not a fan of painstakingly analysing every single calorie for every meal. I'd rather help people get an understanding of what a 'weight loss' and a 'weight maintenance' meal looks for them, so that they automatically make the right choices. Over the years I've honed my skills in understanding nutrition and portion sizes, and making the right choices for me now comes as naturally as breathing. However, when I first start working with clients they usually need some guidelines and parameters to work with, as often they are completely unsure of where and how to begin.

We've done the thinking for you here – these meal plans can help you to work out how to structure your meals, particularly if you are in the process of changing the way you and your family eat. Depending on whether or not you want to lose or maintain weight, feed your growing family or just get healthy, you can adjust as needed. And if you are in weight maintenance mode you won't have to use them all the time – you might just do one for a few days here and there to keep your hand in.

Mish says...

Two things stand out for me with Antoinette. She's organised when it comes to grocery shopping and cooking. And her perspective is 'This is just how we eat'.

ANTOINETTE'S STORY

CASE · · STUDY

The key factor for me keeping the weight off is definitely hands-down the meal plans as you don't have to think about what you can create – it's all there. It's become the norm now and I don't see it as a diet we are trying to stick at – it's just our normal way of eating. I have my husband and children on board too, they are eating healthy and as a bonus my husband has lost 20 kg and counting. We save money by buying just what we need rather than wasting food. It wasn't like we were super unhealthy and eating takeout, having fried foods all the time. I think now it was all the little things just added up, like dressings, sauces and portion sizes. You have taught me how to make spaghetti, chicken curry, lasagne and the beautiful salads in a way that is healthy and so yummy.

STOP STALLING PLAN

This plan is based on a reset calorie count of 1200/day, including the boosters below or snacks (see page 77).

	MONDAY	TUESDAY	WEDNESDAY	THURSDAY	FRIDAY	SATURDAY	SUNDAY
BREAKFAST	Herb and Zucchini Omelette (page 110) 205/serve	Coconut Bircher with Banana (page 112) 285/serve	Oats with Rice Milk and Blueberries (page 78) 254/serve	Herb and Zucchini Omelette (page 110) 205/serve	Coconut Bircher with Banana (page 112) 285/serve	Baked Fruit with Cinnamon Yogurt (page 124) 204/serve	Herb and Zucchini Omelette (page 110) 205/serve
CALORIE BOOSTER	75 g Danish feta 200/serve	extra ½ cup full-cream yoghurt + 2 tbs pumpkin seeds 150/serve	1 tbs slivered almonds + 2 tbs pumpkin seeds 100/serve	100 g avocado 150/serve			1 extra egg yolk 50/serve
LUNCH	Chicken Salad Open Sandwich (page 114) 256/serve	Nourish Bowl (page 118) 267/serve	Chicken Dumpling Soup (from last night) 249/serve	Lentil-stuffed Eggplants (from last night) 274/serve	Honey Mustard Chicken Skewers (page 123) 216/serve	Chicken Salad Open Sandwich (page 114) 256/serve	Lemongrass Beef Salad (from last night) 420/serve
CALORIE BOOSTER	100 g avocado 150/serve	1 extra egg + 1 tbs slivered almonds 150/serve	100 g hokkein noodles 200/serve	25 g tasty cheese 100/serve	2 slices sourdough + 1 tbs sesame seeds 250/serve	100 g avocado 150/serve	1 tbs sesame seeds 50/serve
DINNER	Salmon with Veggie Chips and Basil Pesto (page 120) 299/serve	Chicken Dumpling Soup (page 117; make double batch) 249/serve	Lentil-stuffed Eggplants (page 115; make double batch) 274/serve	Fish Skewers and Fennel Citrus Salad (page 199) 346/serve	Salmon with Veggie Chips and Basil Pesto (page 120) 299/serve	Lemongrass Beef Salad (page 196; make double batch) 420/serve	Nourish Bowl (page 118) 267/serve
CALORIE BOOSTER		100 g cooked peeled prawns 100/serve	25 g tasty cheese 100/serve	200 g steamed cauliflower + 1 tbs slivered almonds 100/serve	180 g cooked sweet potato 150/serve	1 tbs sesame seeds 50/serve	1 x 95 g tin tuna 200/serve
MEAL CALORIES	760	801	777	825	800	880	892
BOOSTER CALORIES	350	400	400	350	400	200	300

SHOPPING LIST
(INCLUDES CALORIE BOOSTERS)

FRESH FRUIT & VEGGIES
- 4 red apples
- 8 cups mixed Asian salad greens
- 2 avocados
- 2 bananas
- 2 cups bean sprouts
- 50 g blueberries
- 6 bulbs baby bok choy
- 2 butter lettuces
- 2 green capsicum
- 5 red capsicum
- 6 carrots
- 200 g cauliflower
- 2 celery stalks
- 2 young coconuts
- 8 baby corn
- 4 Lebanese cucumbers
- 2 telegraph cucumbers
- 10 eggplants
- 3 baby fennel bulbs
- 2 garlic cloves
- 6 cm piece of ginger
- 2 ruby grapefruit
- 200 g green beans
- 3 lemons
- 4 limes
- 2 mandarins
- 2 red onions
- 1 orange
- 2 pears
- 6 cups mixed salad leaves
- 200 g snow peas
- 100 g baby spinach leaves
- 4 spring onions
- 180 g sweet potato
- 4 tomatoes
- 16 zucchini

FRESH HERBS
- basil
- chives
- coriander
- lemon thyme
- mint
- flat-leaf parsley
- 2 lemongrass stalks

BUTCHER
- 1 kg diced lean beef
- 1 kg chicken mince
- 870 g chicken tenderloins

FISHMONGER
- 1.1 kg skinless boneless salmon fillets
- 600 g skinless boneless white fish fillets
- 100 g cooked peeled prawns

DELI/OTHER
- 300 g cherry bocconcini
- 100 g hokkein noodles
- whole egg mayonnaise
- 500 g full-cream unsweetened vanilla yoghurt

PLUS KITCHEN STAPLES
(SEE PAGES 49–50)

SITTING PRETTY PLAN

This plan is based on a maintenance calorie count of 1500/day, including the boosters below or snacks (see page 77).

	MONDAY	TUESDAY	WEDNESDAY	THURSDAY	FRIDAY	SATURDAY	SUNDAY
BREAKFAST	Banoffee Smoothie (page 82) 389/serve	Everyday Porridge (page 130) 342/serve	Sourdough Toast with Avocado and Feta (page 80) 245/serve	Green Toad in the Hole (page 210) 281/serve	Coconut Bircher with Banana (page 112) 285/serve	Salmon-wrapped Asparagus with Avocado Toasts (page 192) 414/serve	Salsa Shakshuka (page 132) 307/serve
CALORIE BOOSTER		½ cup full-cream yoghurt 100/serve	Extra slice of sourdough 100/serve	100 g avocado 150/serve	1 extra banana + extra ½ cup full-cream yoghurt 200/serve		50 g tasty cheese 200/serve
LUNCH	Chicken Nicoise (page 136) 381/serve	Pesto Tuna Wraps (page 131) 458/serve	Bean and Sweet Potato Chilli (from last night) 429/serve	Chicken and Pineapple Rice Salad (from last night) 465/serve	Salmon Crispbreads (page 135) 326/serve	Pea and Cottage Cheese Pie (page 252) 330/serve	Noodle Salad with Prawns (page 195) 335/serve
CALORIE BOOSTER	2 boiled eggs 150/serve	¼ avocado + 50 g cherry bocconcini 150/serve	3 tsp pine nuts 50/serve	75 g feta 200/serve	2 boiled eggs + 3 tsp avocado oil 250/serve	180 g cooked sweet potato 150/serve	¼ avocado + ¼ cup raw cashews 200/serve
DINNER	Baked Italian Cauliflower (page 215) 452/serve	Bean and Sweet Potato Chilli (page 247; make double batch) 429/serve	Chicken and Pineapple Rice Salad (page 202; make double batch) 465/serve	Steak with Bacon and Potato Hash (page 260) 345/serve	Beef and Veggie Lasagne (page 239) 432/serve	Chicken Rissole Parmigiana with Slaw (page 200) 408/serve	Aussie Burger Bowls (page 164) 412/serve
CALORIE BOOSTER	25 g tasty cheese 100/serve		75 g feta 200/serve	1 carrot + ¼ cup baby peas 50/serve		35 g tasty cheese 150/serve	
MEAL CALORIES	1222	1229	1139	1091	1043	1152	1053
BOOSTER CALORIES	250	250	350	400	450	300	400

SHOPPING LIST
(INCLUDES CALORIE BOOSTERS)

FRESH FRUIT & VEGGIES

- 3 bunches asparagus
- 4 avocados
- 4 bananas
- 200 g broccoli florets
- 2 bunches broccolini
- 50 g Brussels sprouts
- 2 green capsicum
- 3 red capsicum
- 9 carrots
- 500 g cauliflower florets
- 4 celery stalks
- 1 young coconut
- 2 × 400 g baby cos
- 6 Lebanese cucumbers
- 1 small eggplant
- 3 garlic cloves
- 100 g seedless green grapes
- 100 g baby green beans
- 1 iceberg lettuce
- 4 large kale leaves
- 5 lemons
- 1 lime
- 2 onions
- 2 red onions
- 1 parsnip
- 100 g sugar snap peas
- 400 g pineapple
- 300 g baby red potatoes
- 85 g baby rocket leaves
- 6 cups mixed salad leaves
- 300 g baby spinach leaves
- 10 spring onions
- 200 g swede
- 1.5 kg sweet potato
- 2 tomatoes
- 200 g mixed baby tomatoes
- 200 g sweet baby tomatoes
- 5 zucchini

FRESH HERBS

- basil
- chives
- coriander
- dill
- mint
- flat-leaf parsley
- rosemary

BUTCHER

- 2 rindless bacon rashers
- 4 × 150 g beef fillet steaks
- 500 g diced 'heart smart' beef
- 500 g extra lean beefburger patties
- 500 g chicken mince
- 8 chicken tenderloins
- 1 kg skinless chicken thigh fillets

FISHMONGER

- 500 g peeled and deveined green (raw) king prawns

DELI/OTHER

- 225 g jar marinated antipasto vegetables
- barbecue sauce
- 5 × 400 g tins four-bean mix
- tinned beetroot
- 200 g cherry bocconcini
- 500 g jar bolognese sauce
- dried herb and garlic breadcrumbs
- 2 burger buns
- caraway seeds
- 150 g tub cashew and basil pesto dip
- 2 ciabatta rolls
- ¼ cup full-fat coconut milk
- ½ cup coconut water
- 16 multigrain crispbreads
- pitted Medjool dates
- 3 fresh lasagne sheets
- 150 g marinated pitted mixed olives
- tinned pineapple rings
- 200 g sliced smoked salmon
- 70 g light sour cream
- 2 × 400 g tins chopped tomatoes with herbs and garlic
- 1 cup full-cream unsweetened vanilla yoghurt
- 2 × 100 g packets dried green bean vermicelli noodles
- Worcestershire sauce

PLUS KITCHEN STAPLES
(SEE PAGES 49–50)

FOOD FOR ONE PLAN

This plan is based on a maintenance calorie count of 1500/day, including the boosters below or snacks (see page 77).

	MONDAY	TUESDAY	WEDNESDAY	THURSDAY	FRIDAY	SATURDAY	SUNDAY
BREAKFAST	Oats with Rice Milk and Blueberries (page 78) 254/serve	Green Toad in the Hole (page 210) 281/serve	Eggs with Asparagus and Carrot (page 80) 182/serve	Granola and Mango Lassi (page 82) 397/serve	Sourdough Toast with Avocado and Feta (page 80) 245/serve	Oats with Rice Milk and Blueberries (page 78) 254/serve	Sourdough Toast with Banana and Honey (page 81) 210/serve
CALORIE BOOSTER	1 tbs slivered almonds + ½ cup full-cream yoghurt 150/serve	100 g avocado + extra 25 g Danish feta 200/serve	2 slices sourdough 200/serve		2 boiled eggs + extra slice sourdough 250/serve	1 tbs slivered almonds + 1 tbs pumpkin seeds + ½ cup full-cream yoghurt 200/serve	Double quantity 210/serve
LUNCH	Pesto Tuna Wraps (page 131) 458/serve	Chicken Dumpling Soup (from last night) 249/serve	Baked Meatballs (from last night) 373/serve	Chicken, Pea and Zucchini Bake (from last night) 387/serve	Lentil, Pea and Ham Soup (from last night) 379/serve	Butter Bean and Salmon Stew (from last night) 273/serve	Everything Meatloaf (from last night) 444/serve
CALORIE BOOSTER	¼ avocado & 2 slices tasty cheese 250/serve	100 g hokkein noodles + 100 g cooked peeled prawns 300/serve	25 g tasty cheese 100/serve	25 g tasty cheese + 1 tbs slivered almonds 150/serve	1 cooked potato + extra 50 g ham 200/serve	1 carrot + ¼ cup baby peas + 25 g goat's cheese 150/serve	100 g avocado + 3 tsp pine nuts 200/serve
DINNER	Chicken Dumpling Soup (page 117) 249/serve	Baked Meatballs (page 170) 373/serve	Chicken, Pea and Zucchini Bake (page 175) 387/serve	Lentil, Pea and Ham Soup (page 150) 379/serve	Butter Bean and Salmon Stew (page 179) 273/serve	Everything Meatloaf (page 263) 444/serve	Miso Chicken with Cucumber and Watercress Salad (page 161) 358/serve
CALORIE BOOSTER	100 g cooked peeled prawns 100/serve	25 g tasty cheese 100/serve	100 g avocado + 1 tbs slivered almonds 200/serve	1 cooked potato + extra 50 g ham 200/serve	1 carrot + ¼ cup baby peas + 25 g goat's cheese 150/serve	100 g avocado + 3 tsp pine nuts 200/serve	2 tbs roasted peanuts 100/serve
MEAL CALORIES	961	903	942	1163	897	971	1012
BOOSTER CALORIES	500	600	500	350	600	550	510

SHOPPING LIST
(INCLUDES CALORIE BOOSTERS)

FRESH FRUIT & VEGGIES

- 1½ bunches of asparagus
- 3 avocados
- 2 bananas
- bean sprouts
- 100 g blueberries
- 3 bulbs baby bok choy
- 300 g broccoli
- 4 carrots
- 3 celery stalks
- 2 corn cobs
- 8 Lebanese cucumbers
- 60 g shelled edamame
- 1 baby fennel bulb
- 5 garlic cloves
- 4 cm piece of ginger
- 200 g green beans
- 1 lime
- 2 onions
- 3 potatoes
- 150 g peeled pumpkin
- 6 cups mixed salad leaves
- 300 g baby spinach leaves
- 2 cups watercress sprigs
- 4 zucchini

FRESH HERBS

- chives
- coriander
- oregano
- flat-leaf parsley
- thyme

BUTCHER

- 100 g white skinless BBQ chicken meat
- 1 kg beef mince
- 500 g chicken mince
- 500 g chicken tenderloins

FISHMONGER

- 200 g cooked peeled prawns
- 100 g skinless boneless salmon fillets

DELI/OTHER

- 150 g tub cashew and basil pesto dip
- 300 g shredded ham
- 100 g hokkein noodles
- 4 small damper rolls
- 2 chicken stock cubes
- 50 g goat's cheese
- tomato ketchup
- roasted peanuts
- ¼ cup dried-fruit-free granola
- frozen mango
- ½ cup coconut water

PLUS KITCHEN STAPLES
(SEE PAGES 49–50)

BULK COOKING PLAN

WEEKEND BATCH COOKING TO DO:
Creamy Chicken and Vegetables (page 232)
Tomato Beans (page 244)

This plan is based on a maintenance calorie count of 1500/day, including the boosters below or snacks (see page 77).

	MONDAY	TUESDAY	WEDNESDAY	THURSDAY	FRIDAY	SATURDAY	SUNDAY
BREAKFAST	Sourdough Toast with Avocado and Feta (page 80) 245/serve	Oats with Rice Milk and Blueberries (page 78) 254/serve	Eggs with Spinach and Mushroom (page 80) 178/serve	Greek Yoghurt with Pumpkin Seeds and Pear (page 79) 265/serve	Sourdough Toast with Avocado and Feta (page 80) 245/serve	Eggs with Spinach and Mushroom (page 80) 178/serve	Everyday Porridge (page 130) 342/serve
CALORIE BOOSTER	Secret Women's Business Smoothie (page 82) 236/serve	½ cup full-cream yoghurt + 2 tbs slivered almonds 200/serve	2 slices sourdough 200/serve	2 tbs slivered almonds 100/serve	Double quantity 245/serve	Apple Pie Smoothie (page 83) 171/serve	½ cup full-cream yoghurt 100/serve
LUNCH	Pesto Tuna Wraps (page 131) 458/serve	Chicken Cottage Pie (from last night) 331/serve	Bean and Sweet Potato Chilli (from last night) 429/serve	Everything Meatloaf (from last night) 444/serve	Chicken Fettuccine (from last night) 461/serve	Lentil, Pea and Ham Soup (page 150) 379/serve	Bean and Eggplant Bake (from last night) 449/serve
CALORIE BOOSTER	2 slices cheese 200/serve	1 tbs mozzarella + 120 g chopped potato 200/serve		100 g avocado + 3 tsp pine nuts 200/serve		1 cooked potato 150/serve	
DINNER	Chicken Cottage Pie (page 234) 331/serve	Bean and Sweet Potato Chilli (page 247) 429/serve	Everything Meatloaf (page 263; make double batch) 444/serve	Chicken Fettuccine (page 235) 461/serve	Salmon with Veggie Chips and Basil Pesto (page 120) 299/serve	Bean and Eggplant Bake (page 247) 449/serve	Fish Skewers and Fennel Citrus Salad (page 199) 346/serve
CALORIE BOOSTER		1 thin slice sourdough 100/serve	100 g avocado + 3 tsp pine nuts 200/serve		extra 3 tsp pine nuts + 180 g cooked sweet potato 200/serve	100 g avocado 150/serve	100 g avocado + 2 tbs almonds 250/serve
MEAL CALORIES	1034	1014	1051	1170	1005	1006	1137
BOOSTER CALORIES	436	500	400	300	445	490	350

SHOPPING LIST (INCLUDES CALORIE BOOSTERS)

FRESH FRUIT & VEGGIES

- 1 red apple
- 1½ avocados
- blueberries
- 600 g broccoli
- 4 green capsicum
- 5 red capsicum
- 11 carrots
- 12 celery stalks
- 4 corn cobs
- 4 Lebanese cucumbers
- 5 eggplants
- 11 baby fennel bulbs
- 9 garlic cloves
- 2 ruby grapefruits
- 100 g seedless green grapes
- 600 g green beans
- 100 g button mushrooms
- 4 onions
- 4 red onion
- 1 orange
- 1 pear
- 1.5 kg potatoes
- 300 g peeled pumpkin
- raspberries
- 10 cups mixed salad leaves
- 500 g baby spinach leaves
- 18 zucchini

FRESH HERBS

- basil
- coriander
- oregano
- 2 bunches flat-leaf parsley

BUTCHER

- 1 kg beef mince
- 2 kg chicken thigh fillets

FISHMONGER

- 700 g skinless boneless salmon fillets
- 300 g skinless boneless white fish fillets

DELI/OTHER

- ½ cup sugar-free apple puree
- 8 x 400 g tins four-bean mix
- 150 g tub cashew and basil pesto dip
- ½ cup coconut water
- 4 × 250 ml tubs '60 per cent less fat' cream for cooking
- 4 small damper rolls
- 200 g dried fettuccine
- 200 g shredded ham
- tomato ketchup

PLUS KITCHEN STAPLES
(SEE PAGES 49–50)

BUILDING A BABY PLAN

This plan is based on a calorie count of 2000/day.
It is recommended to consume double portions of the meals
or single portions with calorie boosters and snacks.

	MONDAY	TUESDAY	WEDNESDAY	THURSDAY	FRIDAY	SATURDAY	SUNDAY
BREAKFAST	Eggs with Asparagus and Carrot (page 80) 182/serve	Smoothie Bowl (page 190) 201/serve	Herb and Zucchini Omelette (page 110) 205/serve	Coconut Bircher with Banana (page 112) 285/serve	Eggs with Spinach and Mushroom (page 80) 178/serve	Coconut Bircher with Banana (page 112) 285/serve	Herb and Zucchini Omelette (page 110) 205/serve
CALORIE BOOSTER	2 slices rye sourdough with butter 300/serve	½ cup full-cream yoghurt + 1 tbs pumpkin seeds + ¼ cup oats 275/serve	100 g avocado + 1 extra egg yolk 200/serve	Extra ½ cup full-cream yoghurt + 2 tbs pumpkin seeds 200/serve	2 slices rye sourdough with butter 300/serve	extra ½ cup full-cream yoghurt 100/serve	1 extra egg yolk + 1 slice sourdough with butter 200/serve
LUNCH	Fish Skewers and Fennel Citrus Salad (page 199) 346/serve	Baked Meatballs (from last night) 373/serve	Chicken, Pea and Zucchini Bake (from last night) 387/serve	Nourish Bowl (page 118) 267/serve	Lemongrass Beef Salad (from last night) 420/serve	Nourish Bowl (page 118) 267/serve	Slow Cooked Beef and Vegetables (page 236) 300/serve
CALORIE BOOSTER	200 g cauliflower florets + extra 100 g fish 250/serve	1 tbs grated mozzarella 50/serve	25 g tasty cheese + 1 tbs slivered almonds 150/serve	1 extra egg + 1 tbs avocado oil 250/serve	¼ cup raw cashews 150/serve	1 x 105 g tin red salmon + 1 tbs avocado oil 300/serve	100 g avocado + 3 tsp pine nuts 200/serve
DINNER	Baked Meatballs (page 170; make double batch) 373/serve	Chicken, Pea and Zucchini Bake (page 175; make double batch) 387/serve	Salmon with Veggie Chips and Basil Pesto (page 120) 299/serve	Lemongrass Beef Salad (page 196; make double batch) 420/serve	Lentil-stuffed Eggplants (page 115) 274/serve	Slow-cooker Chicken Soup (page 217) 375/serve	One-pan Roast Vegetables with Salmon Crumb (page 216) 311/serve
CALORIE BOOSTER	1 tbs grated mozzarella 50/serve	100 g avocado + 1 tbs slivered almonds 200/serve	180 g cooked sweet potato + 3 tsp avocado oil 200/serve	¼ cup raw cashews 150/serve	25 g tasty cheese + ¼ cup cooked brown rice 150/serve	1 extra potato 150/serve	2 extra parsnips + 150 g chicken tenderloins 250/serve
MEAL CALORIES	901	961	891	972	872	927	816
BOOSTER CALORIES	600	525	550	600	600	550	650

SHOPPING LIST
(INCLUDES CALORIE BOOSTERS)

SUGGESTED SNACKS

Almond & Blueberry Jelly (page 144)
91/serve

Greek Yoghurt with Pumpkin Seeds and Pear (page 79)
265/serve

Fierce Greens (page 83)
109/serve

Greek Yoghurt with Almonds and Pomegranate (page 79)
182/serve

Secret Women's Business Smoothie (page 82)
236/serve

Baked Fruit with Cinnamon Yoghurt (page 124)
204/serve

Sourdough Toast with Banana and Honey (page 81)
210/serve

Strawberry Cheesecake Smoothie (page 83)
230/serve

Summer Fruit Salad with Banana Nice Cream (page 206)
169/serve

Oats with Rice Milk and Blueberries (page 78)
254/serve

Greek Yoghurt with Apple Puree and Strawberry (page 79)
167/serve

Fruit-free Granola with Orange (page 79)
290/serve

Banoffee Smoothie (page 82)
389/serve

Granola and Mango Lassi (page 82)
397/serve

Coconut Bircher with Banana (page 112)
285/serve

Watermelon and Lime Ice Pop (page 126)
12/serve

Everyday Porridge (page 130)
342/serve

FRESH FRUIT & VEGGIES

- 2 red apples
- 8 cups mixed Asian salad greens
- ½ bunch of asparagus
- 2½ avocados
- 5 bananas
- 2 beetroots
- 200 g broccoli florets
- 300 g Brussels sprouts
- 2 butter lettuces
- 2 green capsicum
- 4 red capsicum
- 7 carrots
- 200 g cauliflower florets
- 2 celery stalks
- 2 young coconuts
- 8 baby corn
- 2 telegraph cucumber
- 5 eggplants
- 4 bulbs of baby fennel
- 1 whole garlic bulb + 4 garlic cloves
- 2 cm piece of ginger
- 2 ruby grapefruits
- 2 lemons
- 4 limes
- 50 g button mushrooms
- 2 onions
- 2 red onions
- 1 orange
- 5 parsnips
- 2 red-skinned potatoes
- 8 cups mixed salad leaves
- 200 g snow peas
- 130 g baby spinach leaves
- 10 spring onions
- 200 g swede
- 180 g sweet potato
- 10 zucchini

FRESH HERBS

- basil, chives, mint
- 2 stalks lemongrass
- lemon thyme, oregano
- flat-leaf parsley
- rosemary, tarragon

BUTCHER

- 200 g white skinless BBQ chicken meat
- 500 g diced 'heart smart' beef
- 1 kg diced lean beef
- 1 kg beef mince
- 150 g chicken tenderloins
- 400 g skinless chicken thigh fillets

FISHMONGER

- 700 g skinless boneless salmon fillets
- 400 g skinless boneless white fish fillets

DELI/OTHER

- 150 g cherry bocconcini
- caster sugar
- ½ cup coconut water
- 4 small damper rolls
- 400 g tin chopped tomatoes with basil and garlic
- 400 g tin chopped tomatoes with herbs and garlic
- 1 cup full-cream unsweetened vanilla yoghurt

PLUS KITCHEN STAPLES (SEE PAGES 49–50)

BABY BOUNCE-BACK PLAN

This plan is based on a calorie count of 2000/day.
It is recommended to consume double portions of the meals
or single portions with calorie boosters and snacks.

	MONDAY	TUESDAY	WEDNESDAY	THURSDAY	FRIDAY	SATURDAY	SUNDAY
BREAKFAST	Herb and Zucchini Omelette (page 110) 205/serve	Everyday Porridge (page 130) 342/serve	Smoothie Bowl (page 190) 201/serve	Eggs with Asparagus and Carrot (page 80) 182/serve	Green Toad in the Hole (page 210) 281/serve	Smoothie Bowl (page 190) 201/serve	Everyday Porridge (page 130) 342/serve
CALORIE BOOSTER	100 g avocado + 1 extra egg yolk 200/serve	½ cup full-cream yoghurt + 1 tbs slivered almonds 150/serve	½ cup full-cream yoghurt + 2 tbs 100% almond spread 300/serve	1 slice sourdough 100/serve	100 g shredded ham 100/serve	½ cup full-cream yoghurt + 2 tbs 100% almond spread 300/serve	½ cup full-cream yoghurt + 1 tbs slivered almonds 150/serve
LUNCH	Chicken Nicoise (page 136) 381/serve	Everything Meatloaf (from last night) 444/serve	Coconut Prawns and Asian Greens Salad (from last night) 309/serve	Bean and Eggplant Bake (from last night) 449/serve	Chicken and Pineapple Rice Salad (from last night) 465/serve	Salmon Wrapped Asparagus with Avocado Toasts (page 192) 414/serve	Baked Meatballs (from last night) 373/serve
CALORIE BOOSTER	1 extra chicken tenderloin + 3 tsp avocado oil 150/serve	1 slice sourdough with butter 150/serve	1 carrot, 1 zucchini & ½ capsicum 100/serve	100 g avocado 150/serve	75 g feta 200/serve	1 tbs sour cream + 3 tsp avocado oil 150/serve	1 tbs grated mozzarella 50/serve
DINNER	Everything Meatloaf (page 263) 444/serve	Coconut Prawns and Asian Greens Salad (page 203) 309/serve	Bean and Eggplant Bake (page 247) 449/serve	Chicken and Pineapple Rice Salad (page 202) 465/serve	One-pan Roast Vegetables with Salmon Crumb (page 216) 311/serve	Baked Meatballs (page 170) 373/serve	Lentil, Pea and Ham Soup (page 150) 379/serve
CALORIE BOOSTER	1 slice sourdough with butter 150/serve	1 tbs sesame seeds + 1 carrot, 1 zucchini & ½ capsicum 150/serve	100 g avocado 150/serve	75 g feta 200/serve	2 extra parsnips + 1 tbs slivered almonds 150/serve	1 tbs grated mozzarella 50/serve	1 cooked potato + extra 50 g ham 200/serve
MEAL CALORIES	1030	1095	959	1096	1057	988	1094
BOOSTER CALORIES	500	450	550	450	450	500	400

SHOPPING LIST
(INCLUDES CALORIE BOOSTERS)

SUGGESTED SNACKS

Almond & Blueberry Jelly
(page 144)
91/serve

Greek Yoghurt with
Pumpkin Seeds and Pear
(page 79)
265/serve

Fierce Greens
(page 83)
109/serve

Greek Yoghurt
with Almonds and
Pomegranate
(page 79)
182/serve

Secret Women's
Business Smoothie
(page 82)
236/serve

Baked Fruit with
Cinnamon Yoghurt
(page 124)
204/serve

Sourdough Toast with
Banana and Honey
(page 81)
210/serve

Strawberry Cheesecake
Smoothie (page 83)
230/serve

Summer Fruit Salad
with Banana Nice Cream
(page 206)
169/serve

Oats with Rice Milk and
Blueberries (page 78)
254/serve

Greek Yoghurt with
Apple Puree and
Strawberry (page 79)
167/serve

Fruit-free Granola
with Orange (page 79)
290/serve

Banoffee Smoothie
(page 82)
389/serve

Granola and Mango Lassi
(page 82)
397/serve

Coconut Bircher
with Banana (page 112)
285/serve

Watermelon and
Lime Ice Pop (page 126)
12/serve

Everyday Porridge
(page 130)
342/serve

Sourdough Toast with
Avocado and Feta
(page 80)
245/serve

Sourdough Toast with
Cottage Cheese, Tomato
and Basil (page 81)
209/serve

FRESH FRUIT & VEGGIES

- 3½ bunches asparagus
- 3½ avocados
- 6 large bananas
- 2 cups bean sprouts
- 2 beetroot
- 600 g broccoli
- 2 bunches broccolini
- 300 g Brussels sprouts
- 2 green capsicums
- 3 red capsicums
- 10 carrots
- 6 celery stalks
- 2 bunches Chinese broccoli
- 6 bulbs baby choy sum
- 4 corn cobs
- 2 × 400 g baby cos
- 4 eggplants
- 1 garlic bulb + 3 garlic cloves
- 200 g seedless green grapes
- 700 g baby green beans
- 4 lemons
- 2 onions
- 2 red onions
- 4 parsnips
- 400 g peeled pineapple
- 500 g potatoes
- 300 g baby red potatoes
- 300 g peeled pumpkin
- 60 g baby rocket leaves
- 8 cups mixed salad leaves
- 330 g baby spinach leaves
- 8 spring onions
- 10 zucchini

FRESH HERBS

- chives
- coriander
- dill
- lemon thyme
- mint
- oregano
- flat-leaf parsley
- rosemary
- thyme

BUTCHER

- 2 kg beef mince
- 9 chicken tenderloins
- 1 kg skinless chicken thigh fillets

FISHMONGER

- 1.5 kg peeled and deveined green (raw) medium king prawns

DELI/OTHER

- 4 × 400 g tins four-bean mix
- caraway seeds
- 1 cup coconut water
- 4 small damper rolls
- 350 g shredded ham
- 150 g marinated pitted mixed olives
- 200 g sliced smoked salmon
- 1 tablespoon sour cream
- 2 tablespoons mirin
- tomato ketchup

PLUS KITCHEN STAPLES
(SEE PAGES 49–50)

BREAKFAST PROTOCOLS

You hardly have time to eat in the mornings, let alone follow a recipe... I hear you! But you MUST make time for breakfast every day – it's one of the golden rules of a healthy lifestyle. So here's an at-a-glance guide to choosing a simple yet nutritious breakfast option every time. Sweet options are shown here – savoury options are over the page.

CALORIES 254 PER SERVE

+ ½ cup quick oats
+ ½ cup rice milk
+ 50 g blueberries

CALORIES 151 PER SERVE

+ 1 Weet-Bix
+ ½ cup full-fat milk
+ 2 sliced strawberries

CALORIES 279 PER SERVE

+ ½ cup Special K
+ ½ cup soy milk
+ 50 g raspberries

LOW CARB RECIPE
(less than 14 g per serve)

CALORIES
182
PER SERVE

+ ½ cup full-cream unsweetened Greek yoghurt
+ 2 teaspoons toasted slivered almonds
+ 1 tablespoon pomegranate seeds

CALORIES
290
PER SERVE

+ ½ cup dried-fruit-free granola
+ ½ cup unsweetened almond milk
+ ½ peeled segmented orange

CALORIES
265
PER SERVE

+ ½ cup full-cream unsweetened
  Greek yoghurt
+ 1 tablespoon pumpkin seeds
+ ¼ thinly sliced pear

CALORIES
167
PER SERVE

+ ½ cup full-cream unsweetened
  Greek yoghurt
+ 2 tablespoons sugar-free
  apple puree
+ 1 sliced strawberry

79

BREAKFAST PROTOCOLS

CALORIES 245 PER SERVE

+ 1 slice sourdough, toasted
+ ¼ avocado
+ 25 g Danish feta

LOW CARB
RECIPE
(less than 14 g per serve)

CALORIES 178 PER SERVE

+ 2 × 70 g no-oil fried eggs
+ 50 g baby spinach leaves, wilted
+ 50 g grilled button mushrooms

LOW CARB
RECIPE
(less than 14 g per serve)

CALORIES 182 PER SERVE

+ 2 × 70 g boiled eggs
+ 4 asparagus spears
+ ½ carrot, cut into thick sticks

CALORIES
209
PER SERVE

+ 1 thick slice sourdough, toasted
+ ⅓ cup cottage cheese
+ 1 tomato, cut into wedges
+ a few basil leaves

LOW CARB
RECIPE
(less than 14 g per serve)

CALORIES
122
PER SERVE

+ 2 × egg whites and 1 egg no-oil scrambled eggs
+ 20 g shaved leg ham
+ 4 cherry tomatoes or 1 small tomato

CALORIES
210
PER SERVE

+ 1 thick slice sourdough, toasted
+ 1 small sliced banana
+ 2 teaspoons honey

SENSATIONAL SMOOTHIES

Smoothies are quick and delicious and the flavour options are endless (and I've found they're a great way to get nutritious greens into your kids!). You can add the 'To top' options for an extra boost of calories.

GRANOLA AND MANGO LASSI

CALORIES 397 PER SERVE

+ ¼ cup dried-fruit-free granola
+ ⅓ cup full-cream unsweetened Greek yoghurt
+ ½ cup chopped frozen mango
+ ½ cup coconut water

To top:

+ 1 tablespoon finely chopped mango
+ pinch of toasted coconut flakes (11 calories)

BANOFFEE

CALORIES 389 PER SERVE

+ 1 chopped frozen banana
+ 2 pitted Medjool dates
+ ¼ cup full-fat coconut milk
+ ½ cup coconut water
+ ¼ teaspoon ground cinnamon
+ 2 teaspoons pure maple syrup

To top:

+ 3 slices banana
+ ½ teaspoon pure maple syrup (29 calories)

SECRET WOMEN'S BUSINESS

CALORIES 236 PER SERVE

+ 3 brazil nuts
+ 1 cup frozen raspberries
+ ½ cup coconut water
+ 2 teaspoons raw cacao powder
+ ½ teaspoon ground turmeric
+ 2 teaspoons honey

To top:

+ 4 raspberries
+ pinch of raw cacao powder (5 calories)

CALORIES
109
PER SERVE

FIERCE GREENS

+ 2 cups baby spinach leaves
+ ½ teaspoon cayenne pepper
+ 1 peeled kiwi fruit
+ ½ cup ice
+ ½ cup water
+ 3 teaspoons chia seeds
+ ½ cup mint leaves

<u>To top:</u>

+ ¼ teaspoon chia seeds
+ few baby mint leaves
  (4 calories)

CALORIES
171
PER SERVE

APPLE PIE

+ ½ cup cooked quick oats
+ ½ cup sugar-free apple puree
+ ¼ teaspoon ground cinnamon
+ ½ cup unsweetened almond milk
+ ½ cup ice

<u>To top:</u>

+ 1 very thin slice apple
+ 1 teaspoon toasted slivered almonds
  (12 calories)

CALORIES
230
PER SERVE

STRAWBERRY CHEESECAKE

+ 125 g strawberries
+ ¼ cup smooth ricotta
+ ½ cup full-fat milk
+ 1 teaspoon pure vanilla extract
+ 2 teaspoons pure maple syrup
+ few ice cubes

<u>To top:</u>

+ 1 sliced strawberry
  (4 calories)

83

FEEDING THE FAMILY

BREAKFAST

Right, so it's 6.30 am, and you have to provide a healthy, yummy breakfast for the family, taking into account each person's nutritional requirements and tastes. Sounds impossible, I hear you shout? Here's how you do it in 20 minutes from go to whoa.*

DAD

TODDLER

* see over for recipes

MUM

toast

TEENAGER

PRIMARY-SCHOOLER

FEEDING THE FAMILY

BREAKFAST

TOTAL CALORIES FOR DAD 697

TOTAL CALORIES FOR MUM 297

MORNING EGGS

PREP 15 MINUTES | COOK 6 MINUTES

8 eggs

extra light olive oil cooking spray

1 bunch asparagus, trimmed

2 × 250 g punnets cherry tomatoes

1 large avocado

6 slices sourdough, toasted

2 tablespoons butter, at room temperature

1 lemon, cut into wedges

1   Cook the eggs in boiling water for 6 minutes. Drain. Transfer to egg cups on serving plates.

2   Meanwhile, heat a large non-stick frying pan over high heat. Spray with oil. Add the asparagus and 1½ punnets of the tomatoes. Cook, shaking the pan occasionally, for 3 minutes or until the asparagus is just tender and the skins start to split on the tomatoes.

3   Serve the eggs, asparagus and tomatoes with the remaining ingredients as described opposite.

HOW TO SERVE

DAD

+ 2 soft-boiled eggs
+ ⅓ bunch pan-fried asparagus
+ ½ punnet pan-fried cherry toms
+ ¼ avocado, chopped
+ 2 slices sourdough, toasted, spread with 3 teaspoons butter
+ lemon wedges

MUM

+ 1 soft-boiled egg
+ ⅓ bunch pan-fried asparagus
+ ½ punnet pan-fried cherry toms
+ ¼ avocado, chopped
+ ½ slice sourdough, toasted, cut into thick wedges
+ lemon wedges

TEENAGER

+ 2 soft-boiled eggs
+ ⅓ bunch pan-fried asparagus
+ ½ punnet pan-fried cherry toms
+ ¼ avocado, chopped
+ 2 slices sourdough, toasted, spread with 3 teaspoons butter

PRIMARY-SCHOOLER

+ 2 soft-boiled eggs
+ ¼ punnet raw cherry toms, halved
+ ⅛ avocado
+ 1 slice sourdough, toasted, cut in half and spread with 1 teaspoon butter

TODDLER

+ 1 soft-boiled egg
+ ¼ punnet raw cherry toms, halved
+ ⅛ avocado, chopped
+ toast dippers (½ slice sourdough, toasted, cut into fingers) spread with 1 teaspoon butter

GO GREEN

Easy ways to add extra greens at every meal.

BLANCHED
Add broccoli florets to your pan of pasta boiling away for the last 1 minute of cooking.

STIR-FRIED
Separate the leaves of Asian greens and toss in a hot wok, lightly sprayed with extra light olive oil cooking spray, with chopped garlic and ginger for 1 minute, then add a dash of vegetable or chicken stock and stir-fry for a further 1 minute.

TOSSED
Toss baby spinach leaves and coriander leaves through cooked brown basmati rice before serving with your favourite curry or stir-fry.

RAW
Coarsely grate zucchini and toss through your favourite salad combination for extra crunch and sweetness.

SAUTEED
Strip the leaves from a bunch of silverbeet and roughly tear up, then cook in a deep non-stick frying pan over low heat with sliced spring onion and garlic and serve simply with grilled meat or fish.

GRILLED
Pop trimmed asparagus spears onto a lined baking tray and lightly spray with extra light olive oil cooking spray, then sprinkle with cumin seeds, fennel seeds and season to taste. Cook under a hot grill for 2–3 minutes or until just tender and starting to crisp. Serve hot tossed through loads of basil leaves.

CHARRED
Trim kale leaves and wash well, then sprinkle with sesame seeds, a little ground turmeric and ground ginger, then season to taste. Cook on a hot barbecue plate or large chargrill pan for 1 minute each side or until charred and starting to crisp. Remove and serve as an alternative to crackers.

BLENDED
Always add a big handful of baby spinach leaves and tender baby kale leaves to your morning smoothie: they pack a punch in nutrition but are flavourless so are great additions to any smoothie.

OFFICE PANTRY

Here are your go-to options for desk-bound lunches and snacks. Keep a stash of these at your desk for all contingencies.

+ small tins of tuna and salmon

thin rye crispbreads

corn or rice thins

instant miso sachets

+ air-popped popcorn

small tins of beans

+ raw nuts – almonds, brazil nuts, walnuts, cashews and pecans

KEEP IN THE TEAROOM FRIDGE FOR THE WEEK:

+ mini portions of light cream cheese
+ small tubs full-cream unsweetened Greek yoghurt
+ punnets of berries
+ mini shelf-fresh almond milk or full-fat milk portions
+ hummus
+ marinated tofu
+ 50 g portions of shaved deli meat

ON THE GO

If you're anything like me, your handbag is huge and packed with everything bar the kitchen sink to see you through the day. Throw in a couple of these healthy snacks and you'll feel ready to take on anything.

+ cherry tomatoes

+ handful mixed salad leaves

+ mini veggies – baby corn, sugar snap peas, snowpeas

cucumber

+ celery stalks

small piece of fresh fruit –
apple, banana, pear,
orange, mandarin

carrot

FEEDING THE FAMILY

LUNCH

Here's a brilliant way to provide a
healthy lunch for the whole family –
whether to eat *al desko*, in the school
playground or at daycare. The chicken
and eggs can be cooked in advance,
then the night before or the morning
of, get the whole family involved in
the assembly line.*

PRIMARY-SCHOOLER

TEENAGER

TODDLER

* see over for recipes

94

MUM

DAD

FEEDING THE FAMILY

LUNCH

TOTAL CALORIES FOR DAD **1003** TOTAL CALORIES FOR MUM **427**

CHICKEN CAESAR 'SANDWICHES'

PREP 25 MINUTES | COOK 8 MINUTES + COOLING

7 eggs

12 chicken tenderloins, cut in half through the centre lengthways

extra light olive oil cooking spray

4 soft pana di casa rolls, split

3 wholegrain wraps

½ cup whole egg mayonnaise

4 cups mixed salad leaves

50 g parmesan, grated

⅓ cup grated tasty cheese

3 Lebanese cucumbers, 2 peeled into long thin lengths with a vegetable peeler, 1 peeled and sliced

juice of ½ lemon

1 Cook the eggs in boiling water for 8 minutes for hard-boil. Drain. Refresh under cold running water. Peel, then cool. Cut in half lengthways.

2 Meanwhile, heat a large chargrill pan over medium–high heat. Spray the chicken lightly with oil on both sides. Season to taste. Chargrill for 3 minutes each side or until cooked and golden. Remove and cool.

3 Assemble the wraps and rolls with the other ingredients as described opposite.

DAD

(Make rolls)

+ 2 soft pana di casa rolls
+ 8 pieces chicken
  (4 whole tenderloins)
+ 1 cup mixed salad leaves
+ 1 tablespoon mayo
+ 20 g parmesan
+ 2 boiled eggs
+ ½ sliced cucumber

MUM

(Make as a salad)

+ Place half of the salad
  leaves (2 cups) into
  an airtight container
+ 4 pieces chicken
  (2 whole tenderloins)
+ 10 g parmesan
+ 1 boiled egg
+ 1 cucumber
+ lemon juice
+ 1 wrap, packed separately

TEENAGER

(Make rolls)

+ 2 soft pana di casa rolls
+ 8 pieces chicken
  (4 whole tenderloins)
+ 1 cup mixed salad leaves
+ 1 tablespoon mayo
+ 20 g parmesan
+ 2 boiled eggs
+ ½ sliced cucumber

PRIMARY-SCHOOLER

(Placed in separate sections
of a lunchbox)

+ 2 pieces chicken, chopped
  (1 whole tenderloin)
+ 1 wrap spread with 1 tablespoon
  mayonnaise, sprinkled with
  2 tablespoons grated tasty
  cheese then rolled up and cut
  into 2 cm wide pieces
+ 1 boiled egg
+ ½ peeled, sliced cucumber
+ a few salad leaves

TODDLER

(Placed in separate sections
of a lunchbox)

+ 2 pieces chicken, chopped
  (1 whole tenderloin)
+ 1 wrap spread with 1 tablespoon
  mayonnaise, sprinkled with
  2 tablespoons grated tasty
  cheese then rolled up and cut
  into 2 cm wide pieces
+ 1 boiled egg
+ ½ peeled, sliced cucumber

MAKE-AHEAD CHILDREN'S LUNCHBOXES

Here are some clever ideas for lunchboxes that you can make and pack the night before and keep in the fridge. Don't get anxious about providing endless variety – a rotation of three or four options across a school week is more than enough! And don't forget to add plenty of cold or iced reuseable BPA-free water bottles, and small pieces of fruit.

HUMMUS 3 WAYS

Can be made up to four days ahead of serving. Store in an airtight container in the fridge.

Blend 1 × 400 g tin drained and rinsed chickpeas with 1 tablespoon tahini, juice of 1 lemon and:

+ **Avo Hummus** – 1 avocado
+ **Veggie Hummus** – ½ cup leftover cooked veggies (carrot, pumpkin, sweet potato)
+ **Beetroot Hummus** – four slices drained tinned beetroot

SAVOURY WRAPS/ROLL UPS × 3

Use your child's favourite wrap or flat pita bread and fill with:

+ 2 tablespoons spreadable cream cheese, 50 g shaved ham, thinly sliced red and green capsicum
+ ¼ cup basil pesto, 80 g shredded cooked chicken, ¼ cup grated tasty cheese
+ ½ avocado, 1 tablespoon salsa, ½ cup drained, rinsed and patted dry tinned red kidney beans

Then roll up tightly, halve or cut into 4 cm lengths and wrap with plastic wrap.

GREEK YOGHURT STIR-THROUGHS × 3

Place ½ cup full-cream unsweetened Greek yoghurt into small airtight containers. Stir through:

+ ½ peeled kiwi fruit and 2 teaspoons chopped mint, blended until smooth
+ 1 small mashed banana and 1 tablespoon sultanas
+ 50 g mashed raspberries and 2 teaspoons currants

Cover and keep chilled.

MINI QUICHES × 3

Grease and line a mini muffin tray with small squares of puff pastry, then fill with:

+ corn, cream cheese, bacon
+ tuna, tomato, feta
+ ham, cheese, pineapple

Whisk 2 eggs together and pour over filling. Bake in a 200°C (180°C fan-forced) oven for 25 minutes or until cooked, puffed and golden.

MINI QUICHES

BEETROOT HUMMUS

SAVOURY WRAPS/ROLL UPS × 3

+ rice cracker
  + spreadable cream cheese
  + sliced grapes

GREEK YOGHURT STIR-THROUGHS

DIPPERS FOR HUMMUS
+ 50 g crostini and pretzel sticks
+ 1 cup baby veggies – Dutch carrots, baby corn, cukes

FREEZER FILLERS

Having your fresh produce prepped and portioned will save you loads of time when trying to throw something together to eat on busy weeknights. This handy guide outlines the fresh produce most suited to freezing, as well as calorie counts for freezable portions and maximum freezing times.

WARM-WEATHER FRUIT

+ 1 medium peeled and thickly sliced banana [105 calories]	freeze for up to 9 months
+ 1 cup peeled seeded melon: watermelon [50 calories]; honeydew [64 calories]; rockmelon [80 calories]	freeze for up to 9 months
+ 1 cup peeled chopped pineapple [82 calories]	freeze for up to 9 months
+ 1 cup peeled seeded chopped mango [99 calories]	freeze for up to 9 months

COOL-WEATHER FRUIT

+ 1 peeled chopped orange [62 calories]	freeze for up to 3 months
+ 1 sliced seeded pear [57 calories]	freeze for up to 9 months
+ 1 cup grapes [61 calories]	freeze for up to 9 months
+ 1 cup pomegranate seeds (from 1 fruit) [72 calories]	freeze for up to 9 months

WARM-WEATHER VEG

+ 100 g chopped/sliced capsicum [20 calories]	freeze for up to 6 months
+ 100 g chopped/sliced zucchini [20 calories]	freeze for up to 6 months
+ 100 g thickly sliced Asian greens [20 calories]	freeze for up to 6 months
+ 100 g broccolini, cut into 5 cm lengths [20 calories]	freeze for up to 6 months
+ 100 g sweetcorn [80 calories]	freeze for up to 6 months

COOL-WEATHER VEG

+ 100 g chopped carrot [80 calories]	freeze for up to 6 months
+ 100 g peeled, chopped/sliced onion [80 calories]	freeze for up to 6 months
+ 100 g peeled chopped swede [80 calories]	freeze for up to 6 months
+ 100 g peeled chopped turnip [80 calories]	freeze for up to 6 months
+ 100 g peeled, seeded and chopped pumpkin [80 calories]	freeze for up to 6 months
+ 100 g peeled chopped parsnip [80 calories]	freeze for up to 6 months

GRAINS AND BEANS

+ ½ cup cooked brown basmati rice [108 calories]	freeze for up to 3 months
+ 1 cup cooked macaroni [200 calories]	freeze for up to 3 months
+ ½ cup drained tinned beans [100 calories]	freeze for up to 3 months
+ ½ cup drained tinned lentils [100 calories]	freeze for up to 3 months

FISH AND SHELLFISH

+ 150 g fresh white fish [150 calories]	freeze for up to 6 months
+ 150 g fresh peeled deveined prawns [150 calories]	freeze for up to 6 months
+ 100 g fresh salmon [200 calories]	freeze for up to 6 months

POULTRY AND MEAT

+ 100 g chicken [150 calories]	freeze for up to 6 months
+ 100 g red meat [200 calories]	freeze for up to 6 months

TODDLER

PRIMARY-SCHOOLER

TEENAGER

FEEDING THE FAMILY

DINNER

One of my favourite things to do as a family is sit down and eat dinner together at the end of the day. This is pretty hard to manage when you're reheating spag bol for the toddler, barbecuing a steak for your partner and the kids, and throwing together a veggie-packed salad for yourself. Here's a way for you to feed each family member what they want – and need – and not flip your lid.

DAD

see over for recipes

FEEDING THE FAMILY

DINNER

CURRY SPICED LAMB CHOPS WITH MINTY MANGO YOGHURT

PREP 35 MINUTES | COOK 30 MINUTES

12 lamb loin chops

1 tablespoon curry powder

500 g small sweet potatoes, quartered lengthways

500 g cauliflower florets

extra light olive oil cooking spray

500 g green beans, trimmed

4 zucchini, thickly sliced

25 g butter

2 spring onions, thinly sliced

½ cup full-cream unsweetened Greek yoghurt

¼ cup sweet mango chutney

¼ cup mint leaves, finely chopped, plus extra to serve

Shared Salad

4 cups mixed salad leaves (iceberg, butter, cos)

2 Lebanese cucumbers, halved lengthways and thinly sliced diagonally

1 carrot, very thinly sliced into rounds

250 g punnet cherry tomatoes, halved

2 celery stalks, thinly sliced

juice of 1 lemon

1 tablespoon extra virgin olive oil

1 Preheat the oven to 220°C (200°C fan-forced). Line a large baking tray with non-stick baking paper.

2 Coat nine of the lamb chops with curry powder. Season to taste, then season the remaining three chops. Cover and chill until required.

3 Place the sweet potato and cauliflower on the prepared tray. Spray with oil. Season to taste. Bake for 30 minutes, turning twice, or until cooked and golden.

4 Meanwhile, preheat a grill to high. Grill the lamb for 4 minutes each side for medium or cook to your liking. Transfer to a heatproof plate. Cover to rest and keep warm. Steam the beans and zucchini for 5 minutes or until just tender. Transfer to a heatproof bowl. Add the butter and toss until the butter melts. Season to taste. Transfer one-quarter of the vegetables to two serving plates. Add the spring onion to the remaining vegetables in the bowl. Toss to combine. Divide among three serving plates.

5 Using a fork, whisk together the yoghurt, chutney and mint.

6 Make the Shared Salad by tossing all ingredients together in a large serving bowl. Season to taste. Place the salad at the centre of the table for sharing.

HOW TO SERVE

DAD

+ 4 Indian spice-coated
  lamb chops
+ roast sweet potato wedges
  and cauliflower
+ butter blanched green beans,
  zucchini and spring onion
+ minty mango yoghurt
+ Shared Salad
+ extra mint

MUM

+ 2 Indian spice-coated
  lamb chops
+ roast sweet potato wedges
  and cauliflower
+ butter blanched green beans,
  zucchini and spring onion
+ minty mango yoghurt
+ Shared Salad
+ extra mint

TEENAGER

+ 3 Indian spice-coated
  lamb chops
+ roast sweet potato wedges
  and cauliflower
+ butter blanched green beans,
  zucchini and spring onion
+ minty mango yoghurt
+ Shared Salad
+ extra mint

PRIMARY-SCHOOLER

+ 2 lamb chops
+ roast sweet potato wedges
  and cauliflower
+ butter green beans and zucchini,
  no spring onion
+ minty mango yoghurt
+ Shared Salad

TODDLER

+ 1 lamb chop
+ roast sweet potato wedges
  and cauliflower
+ butter green beans and zucchini,
  no spring onion
+ minty mango yoghurt
+ Shared Salad

PART FOUR

THE
RECIPES

RESET RECIPES

These recipes are all under 300 calories per serve, and will get you back on track when you are looking to lose those last few kilos to get to your goal weight. They are also great for those days when you might want to eat a little bit lighter than usual.

HERB AND ZUCCHINI OMELETTE

PREP 10 MINUTES | COOK 20 MINUTES

You can easily make this a gluten-free meal by using your
favourite gluten-free sliced bread.

8 egg whites

4 eggs

½ teaspoon dried tarragon

2 tablespoons chopped chives

1 tablespoon lemon thyme leaves

extra-light olive oil cooking spray

2 zucchini, peeled into long thin lengths
    with a vegetable peeler

4 slices rye sourdough

1   Place the egg whites, eggs, tarragon, chives and lemon
    thyme in a bowl and whisk until foamy and well combined.
    Season to taste.

2   Heat a non-stick frying pan over medium–high heat. Spray lightly
    with oil, making sure to spray the sides of the pan too. Cooking
    in batches, pour one quarter of the egg and herb mixture into
    the pan and tilt it, swirling the mixture to cover the base evenly.
    Cook, untouched, for 3–4 minutes or until set around the edges
    and underneath, but still moist on top. Top with one quarter
    of the zucchini.

3   Using a large, soft spatula, carefully fold half of the omelette
    over to slightly cover the zucchini. Cook, untouched, for 1 minute.
    Slide out of the pan onto a serving plate, covering loosely with
    foil to keep warm. Repeat with the remaining egg and herb
    mixture and zucchini to produce four omelettes.

4   Serve the omelette hot with rye sourdough.

CALORIE BOOST PER SERVE

50 calories	1 extra egg yolk
100 calories	1 extra slice rye sourdough
150 calories	100 g avocado
200 calories	75 g Danish feta

TOTAL CALORIES 821

CALORIES PER SERVE 205

COCONUT BIRCHER WITH BANANA

PREP 15 MINUTES | CHILL OVERNIGHT OR 8 HOURS

Most of the time I use full-cream unsweetened dairy products, as low-fat
alternatives can be loaded with hidden sugars. Always check the label, especially
if you're buying vanilla yoghurt – you want a brand with no added sugar.
And remember a little full-cream dairy goes a long way! You can also make this
a vegan bircher by replacing the yoghurt with a dairy-free alternative.

1 young coconut

1½ cups quick oats

½ cup full-cream unsweetened
 vanilla yoghurt

½ teaspoon ground cinnamon

1 red apple, cored and thinly sliced
 into rounds with a mandolin

1 banana, sliced

1 tablespoon pumpkin seeds

1 tablespoon skinless hazelnuts,
 toasted and halved

1 Remove the top from the coconut and strain out the coconut
 water into a jug (you will need 1¾ cups of coconut water; if you
 don't have enough, just top up with cold tap water).

2 Scoop out the flesh from inside the coconut, then slice. Place
 half the sliced coconut flesh in a large bowl. Place the remaining
 flesh into a resealable food storage bag and chill until required.

3 Add the coconut water, oats, half the yoghurt, the cinnamon and
 apple to the bowl and stir until well combined. Cover and chill
 overnight (or for at least 8 hours).

4 The next morning, add the remaining yoghurt to the bircher
 and stir until well combined. Divide evenly among serving
 bowls and top with the banana, pumpkin seeds, hazelnuts
 and remaining chilled coconut flesh to serve.

CALORIE BOOST PER SERVE

50 calories	extra ¼ cup full-cream unsweetened vanilla yoghurt
100 calories	1 extra banana
150 calories	extra ½ cup quick oats
200 calories	2 slices raisin toast

TOTAL 1140 CALORIES

CALORIES 285 PER SERVE

CHICKEN SALAD OPEN SANDWICH

PREP 10 MINUTES | COOK 8 MINUTES + COOLING TIME

You can make the creamy chicken mixture up to 2 days ahead and store it in an airtight container in the fridge until you're ready to make your sandwich. If you're gluten intolerant, just use your favourite gluten-free sliced bread.

3 chicken tenderloins (185 g)
1 celery stalk, finely chopped
2 tablespoons chopped chives
2 tablespoons whole egg mayonnaise
2 teaspoons dijon mustard
1 tablespoon capers, rinsed
   and finely chopped
4 slices sourdough, toasted
2 tomatoes, sliced
2 cups mixed salad leaves
1 carrot, grated
2 Lebanese cucumbers, peeled
   into long thin lengths

1   Cook the chicken tenderloins in a saucepan of simmering water for 8 minutes or until cooked through. Drain, then cool.

2   Finely chop the chicken and place in a large bowl with the celery, chives, mayonnaise, mustard and capers. Season to taste. Stir until well combined.

3   Place a slice of sourdough on each serving plate and top with the tomato. Add the creamy chicken mixture, salad leaves, carrot and cucumber. Serve.

CALORIE BOOST PER SERVE

50 calories	1 extra chicken tenderloin
100 calories	1 extra slice sourdough
150 calories	100 g avocado
200 calories	2 slices tasty cheese

TOTAL CALORIES 1016

CALORIES PER SERVE 256

DINNER | SERVES 4

LENTIL-STUFFED EGGPLANTS

PREP 15 MINUTES | COOK 12 MINUTES

You can prepare the stuffed eggplants, up to the end of step 3, one day ahead of time. Store in an airtight container in the fridge overnight. The next day, instead of grilling, bake in a preheated 220°C (200°C fan-forced) oven for 15 minutes.

extra-light olive oil cooking spray

4 eggplants, halved lengthways

1 × 400 g tin brown lentils, rinsed and drained

1 × 400 g tin chopped tomatoes with basil and garlic

½ teaspoon dried mixed herbs

50 g baby spinach leaves

150 g cherry bocconcini, torn in half

1 Line a large baking tray with foil and spray lightly with oil. Scoop the flesh from the eggplants, leaving a 5 mm border. Place the eggplant shells on the prepared tray. Chop the eggplant flesh and set aside.

2 Heat a deep frying pan over medium–high heat and spray lightly with oil. Add the chopped eggplant flesh and cook, stirring, for 3 minutes. Add the lentils, tomato and herbs, and cook, stirring, for 5 minutes or until the eggplant is tender. Stir in the spinach until it wilts. Season to taste.

3 Spoon the eggplant and lentil mixture evenly among the eggplant shells. Top with the bocconcini.

4 Preheat the grill to high.

5 Place the stuffed eggplants under the grill for 2 minutes or until the cheese melts and is light golden. Serve.

CALORIE BOOST PER SERVE

50 calories	¼ cup cooked brown basmati rice
100 calories	25 g tasty cheese, grated
150 calories	150 g chicken tenderloin
200 calories	1 cup cooked macaroni

TOTAL CALORIES 1094 | CALORIES PER SERVE 274

LUNCH/
DINNER

SERVES
4

CHICKEN DUMPLING SOUP

PREP 15 MINUTES | COOK 12 MINUTES

You can make the chicken dumplings up to 2 days ahead and store them in an airtight container in the fridge. You can also make the recipe up to the end of step 2, then cool and freeze in an airtight container for up to 3 months. When you're ready to eat, defrost the soup in the fridge overnight, then continue with the recipe from step 3.

500 g chicken mince

1 garlic clove, crushed

2 cm piece of ginger, finely grated

1 tablespoon chopped chives

2 tablespoons chopped coriander leaves, plus small sprigs to garnish

1 litre reduced-salt chicken stock

3 bulbs baby bok choy

2 zucchini, peeled into long thin lengths

1 cup bean sprouts

1 lime, cut into wedges

1   Place the chicken mince, garlic, ginger, chives and chopped coriander in a bowl. Season to taste and mix until well combined. Using slightly damp hands, roll the mixture into walnut-sized balls.

2   Place the chicken dumplings, stock and 1 cup of water in a large saucepan over medium heat. Cook, covered and stirring occasionally, for 10 minutes or until cooked through.

3   Add the bok choy and zucchini to the pan and cook, covered, for a further 2 minutes. Remove from the heat, add the bean sprouts and stir until just combined.

4   Divide the soup among serving bowls, top with the coriander sprigs and serve with the lime wedges.

CALORIE BOOST PER SERVE

50 calories	1 teaspoon sesame oil
100 calories	100 g cooked peeled prawns
150 calories	50 g cooked peeled prawns + 50 g hokkien noodles
200 calories	100 g hokkien noodles

LOW CARB
RECIPE
(less than 14 g per serve)

TOTAL
995
CALORIES

CALORIES
249
PER SERVE

SERVES 4 | LUNCH/DINNER

NOURISH BOWL

PREP 15 MINUTES | COOK 20 MINUTES + COOLING TIME

You can cook the rice and eggs up to 3 days ahead of time and store them in the
fridge. Don't peel the eggs until you are ready to assemble the bowl.
The miso dressing is best made fresh.

½ cup brown basmati rice
4 eggs
4 cups mixed Asian salad greens
½ small red capsicum, seeded and
   finely chopped
100 g snow peas, thinly sliced lengthways
2 spring onions, thinly sliced
4 baby corn, quartered lengthways
1 avocado, sliced
1 tablespoon sesame seeds, toasted
lemon wedges, to serve

Miso dressing

3 teaspoons white miso paste
2 teaspoons apple cider vinegar
1–2 tablespoons warm water

1   Place the rice and 1 cup of water in a saucepan and bring to
    the boil. Reduce the heat and simmer for 15–20 minutes or
    until the rice is just cooked. Drain, then refresh under cold
    running water and drain well again.

2   Meanwhile, cook the eggs in a saucepan of boiling water for
    6 minutes for a soft yolk (or until cooked to your liking). Drain,
    then refresh under cold running water to cool. Peel and cut in
    half lengthways.

3   Meanwhile, make the miso dressing by whisking all the
    ingredients together in a small jug until well combined
    and smooth.

4   Divide the salad greens evenly among serving bowls. Top with
    the rice, capsicum, snow peas, spring onion, corn, avocado and
    egg halves. Sprinkle with sesame seeds and serve with the
    miso dressing.

CALORIE BOOST PER SERVE

50 calories	1 tablespoon slivered almonds
100 calories	1 extra egg
150 calories	1 tablespoon avocado oil
200 calories	1 × 95 g tin tuna with lemon and pepper seasoning

TOTAL CALORIES 1069 | CALORIES PER SERVE 267

SALMON WITH VEGGIE CHIPS AND BASIL PESTO

PREP 20 MINUTES | COOK 35 MINUTES

You can add a little water to the basil pesto to make it a drizzle sauce if you like.

2 carrots, cut into thin chips

1 eggplant, cut into chips

2 zucchini, cut into chips

1 small red capsicum, seeded
    and thickly sliced

extra-light olive oil cooking spray

1 tablespoon finely grated parmesan

4 × 100 g skinless boneless salmon fillets

Basil pesto

1 tablespoon finely grated parmesan

1 cup basil leaves

2 teaspoons red wine vinegar

1 tablespoon pine nuts

1   Preheat the oven to 220°C (200°C fan-forced). Line a large baking tray with non-stick baking paper.

2   Place all the vegetables in a bowl and spray lightly with oil. Add the parmesan, season to taste and toss to coat well. Spread over the prepared tray. Bake for 25 minutes.

3   Remove the baking tray from the oven and add the salmon. Season to taste. Return to the oven and bake for 10 minutes.

4   Meanwhile, make the basil pesto. Place all the ingredients in a small food processor and blend until well combined and smooth. Add a little water to loosen if needed. Season to taste.

5   Divide the veggie chips and salmon among serving plates. Top with the basil pesto and serve.

CALORIE BOOST PER SERVE

50 calories	extra 3 teaspoons pine nuts
100 calories	3 teaspoons avocado oil
150 calories	180 g cooked sweet potato
200 calories	extra 100 g skinless boneless salmon fillet

LOW CARB
RECIPE
(less than 14 g per serve)

TOTAL
1197
CALORIES

CALORIES
299
PER SERVE

DINNER | SERVES 4

HONEY MUSTARD CHICKEN SKEWERS

PREP 15 MINUTES | COOK 15 MINUTES

You can marinate the chicken for up to 2 days
ahead of cooking. Store in an airtight container in the fridge.

500 g chicken tenderloins
1 tablespoon wholegrain mustard
1 tablespoon honey
extra-light olive oil cooking spray
200 g green beans, trimmed
2 zucchini, thickly sliced
200 g cauliflower florets
1 small lemon, cut into wedges
2 cups mixed salad leaves

1   Heat a barbecue or large chargrill pan over medium heat.

2   Place the chicken, mustard and honey in a bowl. Season to taste and stir well to coat. Thread the chicken, lengthways, onto skewers and spray lightly with oil on both sides.

3   Chargrill the chicken skewers for 12–15 minutes, turning occasionally or until cooked through and golden.

4   Meanwhile, bring a large saucepan of water to the boil. Add the green beans, zucchini and cauliflower and blanch for 2 minutes. Drain well, then return to the pan and spray lightly with oil. Season to taste.

5   Serve the chicken skewers with the vegetables, salad leaves and lemon wedges.

CALORIE BOOST PER SERVE

50 calories	1 tablespoon sesame seeds
100 calories	extra 100 g chicken tenderloin
150 calories	2/3 cup cooked egg noodles
200 calories	2 thin slices sourdough

LOW CARB
RECIPE
(less than 14 g per serve)

TOTAL **865** CALORIES

CALORIES **216** PER SERVE

BAKED FRUIT WITH CINNAMON YOGHURT

PREP 10 MINUTES | COOK 30 MINUTES

You can make this up to 1 day ahead of serving. Store the fruit and yoghurt separately in airtight containers in the fridge. Reheat the fruit in a microwave on medium heat for 2–3 minutes to warm.

2 red apples, each cut into 6 wedges
   and cored
2 pears, quartered and cored
2 mandarins, peeled and halved widthways
juice of 1 lemon
1 cinnamon stick, broken in half
½ cup (125 ml) boiling water
2 tablespoons pumpkin seeds, toasted

Cinnamon yoghurt

¾ cup full-cream unsweetened
   vanilla Greek yoghurt
½ teaspoon ground cinnamon

1   Preheat the oven to 200°C (180°C fan-forced).

2   Place the apple, pear, mandarin, lemon juice, cinnamon and boiling water in a deep baking dish. Cover tightly with foil. Bake for 30 minutes or until the fruit is tender.

3   Make the cinnamon yoghurt by combining the ingredients together until smooth. Chill until required.

4   Serve the warm fruit with the pan juices and cinnamon yoghurt, scattered with the toasted pumpkin seeds.

TOTAL CALORIES 816

CALORIES PER SERVE 204

WATERMELON AND LIME ICE POP

PREP 10 MINUTES | FREEZE 6 HOURS

You can store these ice pops in the freezer for up to 6 months.

1½ cups chopped seedless watermelon
juice of 1 lime
¼ cup small mint leaves

1   Blend the watermelon and lime juice together in a blender until smooth. Stir through the mint leaves.

2   Pour the mixture evenly into six ½ cup capacity ice-pop moulds and insert wooden sticks. Freeze for 6 hours or until firm.

LOW CARB
RECIPE
(less than 14 g per serve)

TOTAL
108
CALORIES

CALORIES
18
PER SERVE

FIVE INGREDIENT PANTRY PLUS

You don't have to spend loads of money or use twenty different ingredients to create delicious meals. Here I show you how to do it using just FIVE ingredients for each recipe – a mix of pantry staples and beautiful fresh produce.

EVERYDAY PORRIDGE

Oats + milk + craisins + pumpkin seeds + grapes

PREP 5 MINUTES | COOK 3 MINUTES

You can use your favourite milk of choice here –
almond, rice or coconut all work well.

2 cups quick oats

2 cups milk

⅓ cup craisins

¼ cup pumpkin seeds

100 g seedless green grapes, sliced

1 Place the oats, milk and 1 cup of water in a saucepan over medium heat. Cook, stirring occasionally, for 3 minutes or until the oats are tender and the mixture thickens slightly.

2 Stir through the craisins. Remove the pan from the heat.

3 Divide the porridge among serving bowls and top with the pumpkin seeds and grapes. Serve.

CALORIE BOOST PER SERVE

50 calories	3 teaspoons pure maple syrup
100 calories	½ cup full-cream unsweetened vanilla yoghurt
150 calories	½ cup full-cream unsweetened vanilla yoghurt + 1 tablespoon slivered almonds
200 calories	2 slices raisin toast

TOTAL 1368 CALORIES

CALORIES 342 PER SERVE

LUNCH | SERVES 4

PESTO TUNA WRAPS

Tuna + rye mountain bread + pesto dip + cucumber + salad leaves

PREP 10 MINUTES

You need to work very quickly when using mountain bread wraps as they can dry out and crack. If you're preparing these ahead of time for transporting, double up two of the wraps before filling and wrap them tightly in plastic film.

1 × 425 g tin tuna in springwater, drained

8 rye mountain bread wraps

1 × 150 g tub cashew and basil pesto dip

4 Lebanese cucumbers, peeled into long thin lengths

2 cups mixed salad leaves

1 Divide the tuna among the wraps and top with the pesto dip, cucumber and salad leaves. Season to taste.

2 Working quickly, fold in the ends of each wrap and roll up. Cut in half crossways to serve.

CALORIE BOOST PER SERVE

50 calories	¼ avocado
100 calories	50 g cherry bocconcini
150 calories	180 g cooked sweet potato
200 calories	2 slices tasty cheese

TOTAL CALORIES 1831 | CALORIES PER SERVE 458

SALSA SHAKSHUKA

Four-bean mix **+** salsa **+** kale **+** eggs **+** sourdough

PREP 5 MINUTES | COOK 20 MINUTES

You can add a good pinch of dried chilli flakes to bring a little spice, if desired.

1 × 400 g tin four-bean mix
2 × 300 g jars mild chunky salsa
4 large kale leaves, stems removed,
    leaves shredded
4 eggs
4 slices rye sourdough, toasted

1   Place the beans, salsa, kale and 1 cup of water in a deep
    frying pan over medium heat. Cook, stirring occasionally,
    for 15 minutes or until the kale wilts and the mixture reduces
    slightly. Season to taste.

2   Using the back of a large knife or spoon, make four wells in the
    mixture. Crack an egg into each well, being careful not to break
    the yolk. Cook, untouched, for 5 minutes or until the egg whites
    are set and the yolks still runny.

3   Serve with toasted sourdough.

CALORIE BOOST PER SERVE

50 calories	3 teaspoons pine nuts
100 calories	1 extra slice sourdough
150 calories	180 g cooked sweet potato
200 calories	50 g tasty cheese, grated

TOTAL 1226 CALORIES

CALORIES 307 PER SERVE

BRUNCH/ LUNCH

SERVES 4

SALMON CRISPBREADS

Crispbread **+** tinned salmon **+** tomato **+** rocket **+** lemon

PREP 10 MINUTES

This is a great one for your lunchbox. Store the salmon mixture separately in an airtight container and keep chilled until serving.

16 multigrain crispbreads
1 × 415 g tin pink salmon, drained
200 g sweet baby tomatoes, sliced
25 g baby rocket leaves
1 lemon, halved

1   Divide the crispbreads among serving plates.

2   Place the salmon in a bowl and roughly mash with a fork. Add the tomato and rocket, and squeeze over the juice from half the lemon. Season to taste. Stir until well combined, then spoon over the crispbreads.

3   Cut the remaining lemon half into wedges and serve alongside.

CALORIE BOOST PER SERVE

50 calories	1 extra crispbread
100 calories	3 teaspoons avocado oil
150 calories	2 boiled eggs
200 calories	⅓ cup reduced-fat spreadable cream cheese

TOTAL CALORIES 1305

CALORIES PER SERVE 326

SERVES 4

LUNCH/ DINNER

CHICKEN NICOISE

Baby potatoes **+** green beans **+** chicken **+** cos **+** marinated olives

PREP 10 MINUTES | COOK 25 MINUTES + COOLING + 5 MINUTES RESTING

You can cook the potatoes, beans and chicken up to 1 day ahead of serving. Store them separately in airtight containers in the fridge.

300 g baby red potatoes, halved
100 g baby green beans, trimmed
8 chicken tenderloins
2 × 400 g baby cos, trimmed
    and leaves separated
150 g marinated pitted
    mixed olives

1   Cook the potatoes in a saucepan of boiling water for 12 minutes. Add the beans and cook for a further 1 minute. Drain, then cool.

2   Heat a large chargrill pan over medium–high heat. Chargrill the chicken for 12 minutes, turning occasionally, or until cooked and golden. Transfer to a heatproof chopping board. Rest for 5 minutes before slicing.

3   Place the cos, olives (and their marinade), potatoes, beans and chicken in a large bowl. Season to taste. Toss gently together to combine, then serve.

CALORIE BOOST PER SERVE

50 calories	1 extra chicken tenderloin
100 calories	3 teaspoons avocado oil
150 calories	2 boiled eggs
200 calories	2 thin slices sourdough

LOW CARB
RECIPE
(less than 14 g per serve)

TOTAL 1523 CALORIES

CALORIES 381 PER SERVE

CHICKEN KORMA PILAF

Korma curry paste + chicken + brown rice + baby spinach leaves + slivered almonds

PREP 10 MINUTES | COOK 25 MINUTES

Leftovers are perfect for lunch the next day. Store in an airtight container and keep
chilled. Simply reheat in a microwave on medium for 2–3 minutes.

¼ cup korma curry paste
500 g chicken breast fillet, chopped
2 × 250 g packets microwave steamed
   brown basmati rice
100 g baby spinach leaves
⅓ cup slivered almonds, toasted

1   Cook the curry paste in a large saucepan over low heat for
    3 minutes or until fragrant. Increase the heat to medium
    and add the chicken. Cook, stirring, for 10 minutes or until
    cooked through.

2   Add the rice and 1 cup of water, then stir well. Cook, covered,
    for 10 minutes or until the water has been absorbed and the
    rice is fluffy. Add the spinach and stir until almost wilted.

3   Divide the pilaf among serving bowls, top with the almonds
    and serve.

CALORIE BOOST PER SERVE

50 calories	1 extra tablespoon toasted slivered almonds
100 calories	½ cup full-cream unsweetened Greek yoghurt
150 calories	4 cooked pappadums
200 calories	1 naan bread

TOTAL CALORIES 1528

CALORIES PER SERVE 382

DINNER | SERVES 4

TOFU SATAY

Coconut milk **+** peanut butter **+** marinated tofu **+** bok choy **+** carrot

PREP 10 MINUTES | COOK 20 MINUTES

You can make the satay sauce up to 2 days ahead of serving. Store in an airtight container in the fridge and reheat in a saucepan over low heat, adding a little water to loosen if necessary.

1 × 270 ml tin light coconut milk
¼ cup crunchy peanut butter
1 × 200 g packet Malaysian marinated tofu, halved diagonally
6 bulbs baby bok choy, halved lengthways
2 carrots, sliced into matchsticks

1 Place the coconut milk and peanut butter in a small saucepan over low heat. Cook, stirring occasionally, for 10 minutes or until well combined and hot. Keep the satay sauce warm.

2 Meanwhile, heat a large chargrill pan over medium–high heat.

3 Chargrill the tofu and bok choy, in two separate batches, for 5 minutes each or until just cooked and golden. Transfer to a large bowl and add the carrot. Toss to combine.

4 Divide the tofu mixture evenly among serving plates and serve with the satay sauce.

CALORIE BOOST PER SERVE

50 calories	1 tablespoon roasted peanuts
100 calories	50 g extra Malaysian marinated tofu
150 calories	⅔ cup cooked egg noodles
200 calories	100 g hokkien noodles

LOW CARB
RECIPE
(less than 14 g per serve)

TOTAL CALORIES 1053 | CALORIES PER SERVE 263

141

ANTIPASTO CRISPY-SKIN CHICKEN

Feta-stuffed green olives + marinated artichoke + zucchini + tomato + chicken

PREP 10 MINUTES | COOK 40 MINUTES

This dish travels well and is perfect for picnics. Simply transport
in an airtight, watertight container and keep chilled. I use
97 per cent fat-free marinated artichoke hearts here.

200 g feta-stuffed green olives

1 × 170 g jar marinated artichoke
hearts, undrained

4 zucchini (600 g), sliced into rounds

200 g baby mixed tomatoes

4 chicken thigh cutlets (500 g), with skin on

1 Preheat the oven to 200°C (180°C fan-forced). Line a baking tray with non-stick baking paper.

2 Combine all the ingredients together in a large bowl. Season to taste. Toss well to coat.

3 Transfer the chicken to the prepared tray, placing it skin-side up. Bake for 20 minutes.

4 Remove the chicken from the oven and add all the remaining ingredients to the tray, making sure the chicken sits on top of the mixture, skin-side up.

5 Bake for 20 minutes or until the chicken is cooked and the skin is crispy. Serve.

CALORIE BOOST PER SERVE

50 calories	3 teaspoons pine nuts
100 calories	50 g cherry bocconcini
150 calories	1 slice garlic bread
200 calories	1 cup cooked macaroni

LOW CARB
RECIPE
(less than 14 g per serve)

TOTAL CALORIES 1510

CALORIES PER SERVE 378

ALMOND AND BLUEBERRY JELLY

Almond milk + gelatine + maple syrup + vanilla + blueberries

PREP 10 MINUTES | COOK 2 MINUTES | CHILL 4 HOURS

You can make these puddings up to 2 days ahead of serving. Cover and keep chilled.

1 litre unsweetened almond milk, chilled

1 tablespoon powdered gelatine

1 tablespoon pure maple syrup, plus extra syrup to serve

1 teaspoon pure vanilla extract

125 g blueberries

1   Place half of the milk in a small saucepan over low–medium heat. Bring to a simmer, then immediately remove from the heat and whisk in the gelatine. Continue whisking until the gelatine dissolves.

2   Whisk in the maple syrup, vanilla and remaining chilled milk until well combined. Pour the mixture evenly into four 300 ml capacity serving glasses or dishes.

3   Chill for 2 hours or until slightly set. Top with the blueberries. Chill for a further 2 hours or until set firm. Serve chilled with extra blueberries and a drizzle of maple syrup.

LOW CARB
RECIPE
(less than 14 g per serve)

TOTAL CALORIES 364

CALORIES PER SERVE 91

RASPBERRY CHEESECAKE FINGERS

Savoiardi **+** cream cheese **+** raspberries **+** dark chocolate **+** maple syrup

PREP 10 MINUTES

You can swap the raspberries for blueberries, strawberries or a combination of all three berries if you like. One serve consists of two cheesecake fingers.

8 (about 100 g) Savoiardi sponge fingers
½ cup extra-light spreadable cream cheese
125 g raspberries
5 g dark chocolate (90 per cent cocoa)
2 teaspoons pure maple syrup

1 Place the sponge fingers on a serving plate, flat-side up.

2 Spread the cream cheese evenly over the sponge fingers.

3 Top with the raspberries, then finely grate the chocolate over the top. Drizzle with maple syrup. Serve immediately.

TOTAL CALORIES 582

CALORIES PER SERVE 146

TIME-SAVER DINNERS

Want to feed your family well, but short on time? All these meals cook in 15 minutes, using clever shortcuts that prove you *can* have convenient, 'fast' food that is good for you.

LENTIL, PEA AND HAM SOUP

PREP 5 MINUTES | COOK 15 MINUTES

You can buy shredded ham from the deli counter of supermarkets and greengrocers.

1 × 400 g tin brown lentils,
  drained and rinsed

1 garlic clove, crushed

2 celery stalks, thinly sliced

4 sprigs thyme

200 g shredded ham

1 litre salt-reduced chicken stock

1 cup frozen baby peas

4 small damper rolls

1   Place the lentils, garlic, celery, thyme, ham, stock and 2 cups water in a large saucepan over high heat. Cook, covered, for 12 minutes, stirring occasionally.

2   Stir in the peas and cook for a further 2 minutes or until heated through. Season to taste.

3   Serve the soup with the damper rolls.

CALORIE BOOST PER SERVE

50 calories	extra 50 g shredded ham
100 calories	25 g goat's cheese
150 calories	1 cooked potato, chopped
200 calories	50 g cooked chorizo

TOTAL 1517 CALORIES

CALORIES 379 PER SERVE

BAKED SOY AND GINGER FISH

PREP 15 MINUTES | COOK 15 MINUTES

If you like, you can swap the salmon in this recipe for chicken
tenderloins – just halve them lengthways. Check the marinade
label and go for the one with the lowest sugar content.

⅓ cup soy, honey and garlic marinade

3 cm piece of ginger, finely grated

4 × 100 g skinless boneless salmon fillets,
  halved lengthways

1 × 125 g packet baby corn,
  halved lengthways

150 g sugar snap peas, trimmed

100 g snow peas, trimmed

1 small red capsicum, seeded
  and sliced

1 × 250 g packet microwave jasmine rice

1 cup small basil leaves

1 Preheat the oven to 220°C (200°C fan-forced) and line a large
  baking tray with baking paper.

2 Place the marinade, ginger, salmon, corn, sugar snap peas,
  snow peas, capsicum and ⅓ cup of water in a large bowl and
  toss gently to combine. Spread the mixture evenly over the
  prepared tray.

3 Bake for 12 minutes or until the salmon and vegetables are
  just tender.

4 Meanwhile, heat the rice according to the packet instructions.

5 Serve the salmon and vegetables scattered with basil, with
  the rice alongside.

CALORIE BOOST PER SERVE

50 calories	1½ teaspoons sesame oil
100 calories	80 g cooked sweet potato
150 calories	¼ cup raw unsalted cashews
200 calories	extra 100 g skinless boneless salmon fillet

TOTAL CALORIES 1563

CALORIES PER SERVE 391

STACKED BEEF TORTILLAS WITH AVOCADO SALAD

PREP 15 MINUTES | COOK 5 MINUTES

The fun part about these tortillas is that there is *way* too much filling to be able to roll them up, making it a joyful, messy experience that the kids will love! If you have time, you can marinate the steaks in the spice mix overnight – just cover them and keep them chilled until cooking. I use 33 per cent reduced-fat light tortillas here.

1 × 450 g packet beef schnitzel steak
1 × 40 g packet burrito spice mix
extra-light olive oil cooking spray
4 light tortillas
½ small iceberg lettuce, chilled, thinly shredded
1 × 300 g jar mild salsa

Avocado salad

1 avocado, sliced
2 Lebanese cucumbers, halved lengthways and thinly sliced diagonally
1 cup small coriander sprigs
juice of 1 lemon

1 Preheat a large chargrill pan over medium–high heat.

2 Make the avocado salad by gently tossing all the ingredients together until well combined. Season to taste.

3 Sprinkle the steak with the spice mix on both sides to coat evenly, then spray lightly with oil. Chargrill for 1 minute on each side or until just cooked and golden. Slice into 8 pieces and then transfer to a heatproof plate and cover loosely with foil to keep warm.

4 Spray the tortillas lightly with oil on both sides. Chargrill, in two separate batches, for 5 seconds on each side or until heated and golden. Transfer to serving plates.

5 Top the tortillas evenly with the iceberg, steaks, salsa and avocado salad. Serve.

CALORIE BOOST PER SERVE

50 calories	extra ¼ avocado
100 calories	1 extra tortilla
150 calories	¼ cup sour cream
200 calories	50 g tasty cheese, grated

TOTAL CALORIES 1630

CALORIES PER SERVE 408

TUNA, PEA AND RAVIOLI TOSS

PREP 5 MINUTES | COOK 15 MINUTES

Make sure you go for a good-quality pasta sauce with no added
sugar. This is another brilliant one for your lunchbox. Keep chilled,
then reheat in a microwave on medium for 2–3 minutes.

1 × 200 g packet fresh mini ravioli
   with cheese and vegetables
1 × 425 g tin tuna in springwater
1 × 500 g jar napoletana pasta sauce
1 cup frozen baby peas
30 g parmesan, finely grated
mixed salad leaves, to serve

1   Cook the ravioli in a saucepan of boiling water for 6–10 minutes
    until tender. Drain, reserving ½ cup of the cooking water.

2   Return the same pan to high heat. Add the tuna, sauce and peas.
    Cook, stirring, for 2–3 minutes until hot. Add the ravioli and just
    enough of the reserved cooking water to loosen the mixture.
    Stir until well combined. Season to taste.

3   Divide the ravioli among serving bowls and top with parmesan.
    Serve with salad leaves.

CALORIE BOOST PER SERVE

50 calories	1 carrot + extra ¼ cup baby peas
100 calories	25 g tasty cheese, grated
150 calories	extra 50 g fresh mini ravioli with cheese and vegetables
200 calories	1½ slices garlic bread

TOTAL CALORIES 1245

CALORIES PER SERVE 311

SERVES 4

HONEY AND LEMON CHICKEN STIR-FRY

PREP 10 MINUTES + 5 MINUTES STANDING | COOK 8 MINUTES

For a vegetarian option, swap the chicken for firm tofu.

1 × 450 g packet fresh thin hokkien noodles

400 g chicken breast fillets, thinly sliced

3 bulbs baby bok choy, leaves separated

1 carrot, halved lengthways and thinly sliced diagonally

juice of 1 lemon

2 tablespoons honey

1 garlic clove, crushed

2 spring onions, thinly sliced diagonally

1   Place the noodles in a large heatproof bowl and cover with boiling water. Leave for 5 minutes or until the noodles easily separate. Drain well.

2   Meanwhile, heat a large non-stick wok over high heat. Add the chicken and stir-fry for 5 minutes or until cooked and light golden. Add the bok choy, carrot, lemon juice, honey, garlic and ¼ cup of water, and stir-fry for 2 minutes.

3   Add the drained noodles to the wok. Stir-fry for 1 minute or until well combined with the chicken mixture. Remove the wok from the heat.

4   Add half the spring onion and toss gently to combine.

5   Divide among serving bowls, top with the remaining spring onion and serve.

CALORIE BOOST PER SERVE

50 calories	1½ teaspoons sesame oil
100 calories	100 g cooked peeled prawns
150 calories	50 g cooked peeled prawns + extra 50 g hokkien noodles
200 calories	extra 100 g hokkien noodles

TOTAL CALORIES 1326 | CALORIES PER SERVE 332

MISO CHICKEN WITH CUCUMBER AND WATERCRESS SALAD

PREP 15 MINUTES | COOK 7–10 MINUTES

You'll find shelled edamame (soy beans) in the frozen vegetable aisle in Asian grocery stores and some large supermarkets. There's no need to thaw the edamame before grilling – they will cook perfectly in the time provided.

extra-light olive oil cooking spray
2 tablespoons white miso paste
2 cm piece of ginger, finely grated
½ teaspoon sesame oil
¼ cup mirin
500 g chicken tenderloins, halved
   through centre
1 cup shelled edamame
2 tablespoons sesame seeds, toasted

Cucumber and watercress salad

4 Lebanese cucumbers, very thinly sliced
2 cups watercress sprigs
¼ cup mirin
2 tablespoons finely chopped chives

1   Preheat the grill to high. Line a large baking tray with foil and spray lightly with oil.

2   Place the miso, ginger, sesame oil, mirin, chicken and edamame in a large bowl. Season with freshly ground black pepper. Stir until well combined and coated.

3   Spread the mixture evenly over the prepared tray and spray lightly with oil. Cook under the grill for 7–10 minutes until cooked and golden.

4   Meanwhile, make the cucumber and watercress salad by combining the cucumber, mirin and salt and pepper to taste. Leave to stand for 5 minutes then add the remaining ingredients and toss to combine.

5   Divide the salad among serving plates and sprinkle with sesame seeds. Serve alongside the grilled chicken mixture.

CALORIE BOOST PER SERVE

50 calories	1 extra chicken tenderloin
100 calories	2 tablespoons roasted peanuts
150 calories	100 g avocado
200 calories	100 g hokkien noodles

TOTAL CALORIES 1432

CALORIES PER SERVE 358

161

BBQ CHICKEN NACHOS

PREP 10 MINUTES | COOK 2 MINUTES

Depending on your family's personal taste, you can of
course remove the coriander if needed!

1 × 425 g tin black beans, drained and rinsed

200 g white skinless BBQ chicken meat,
   thinly shredded

50 g mozzarella, finely grated

1 × 300 g jar mild chunky salsa

1 carrot, sliced

2 Lebanese cucumbers, sliced

½ cup coriander leaves

50 g unsalted baked corn chips

1   Preheat the grill to high.

2   Spread the beans evenly over four heatproof serving plates.
    Top with the chicken, then the cheese. Cook under the grill
    for 2 minutes or until the cheese melts and is light golden.

3   Top the hot bean mixture with the salsa, then the carrot,
    cucumber and coriander. Serve with corn chips alongside.

CALORIE BOOST PER SERVE

50 calories	extra 1 tablespoon finely grated mozzarella
100 calories	2 tablespoons sour cream
150 calories	extra 25 g unsalted baked corn chips
200 calories	extra 150 g white skinless BBQ chicken meat

TOTAL 1193 CALORIES | CALORIES 298 PER SERVE

AUSSIE BURGER BOWLS

PREP 10 MINUTES | COOK 12 MINUTES

You can easily make this a vegetarian or vegan meal by swapping
the beef patties for a meat-free pattie. Check the barbecue sauce
label and choose the brand with the lowest sugar content.

500 g extra lean beefburger patties

1 onion, thinly cut into rings

4 iceberg lettuce leaves, shredded

2 tomatoes, sliced

4 tinned pineapple rings, drained

8 small slices tinned beetroot

⅓ cup barbecue sauce

2 burger buns, split and toasted

1 Heat a large non-stick frying pan over medium–high heat.
   Add the burger patties and onion. Cook, turning occasionally,
   for 10–12 minutes until cooked and golden.

2 Meanwhile, divide the lettuce evenly among serving bowls
   and top with the tomato, pineapple and beetroot.

3 Add the cooked patties and onion to the salad mixture. Drizzle
   with barbecue sauce and serve with the halved buns.

CALORIE BOOST PER SERVE

50 calories	1 extra tablespoon barbecue sauce
100 calories	1 slice tasty cheese
150 calories	75 g short cut bacon, cooked
200 calories	1 extra burger bun

TOTAL CALORIES 1647   CALORIES PER SERVE 412

CHICKPEA AND VEGGIE CURRY

PREP 5 MINUTES | COOK 15 MINUTES

This curry is even more delicious if you make it the day before serving, as the flavours really develop overnight.

1 × 420 g jar korma simmer sauce

1 × 400 g tin chickpeas, drained and rinsed

1 red onion, cut into thin wedges

1 carrot, thinly sliced

200 g small cauliflower florets

100 g green beans, trimmed and
   halved crossways

2 pieces garlic and herb naan,
   halved and heated

1   Place the korma sauce, chickpeas, onion, carrot, cauliflower and 1 cup of water in a saucepan over high heat. Cook, stirring occasionally, for 12 minutes or until the vegetables are just tender.

2   Stir in the beans and cook for a further 2 minutes or until the beans are bright green.

3   Serve the curry with the warm garlic and herb naan.

CALORIE BOOST PER SERVE

50 calories	1½ tablespoons full-cream unsweetened Greek yoghurt
100 calories	extra ½ piece naan
150 calories	180 g cooked sweet potato
200 calories	¾ cup cooked brown basmati rice + 1½ tablespoons slivered almonds

TOTAL 1580 CALORIES

CALORIES 395 PER SERVE

SERVES
4

KOREAN BEEF

PREP 10 MINUTES | COOK 10 MINUTES

You can swap the beef mince for chicken mince or kangaroo mince if preferred. Kangaroo meat is a great low-calorie, low-fat source of all the nutrients you'd expect from a red meat.

500 g beef mince

2 garlic cloves, crushed

4 cm piece of ginger, finely grated

1 long red chilli, seeded and thinly sliced

½ teaspoon sesame oil

¼ cup tamari (gluten-free soy sauce)

4 spring onions, thinly sliced

2 × 250 g packets microwave
  long-grain white rice

1 large butter lettuce, leaves separated

1   Heat a large non-stick frying pan over high heat. Add the mince. Cook, breaking up any lumps with the back of a spoon, for 5 minutes. Add the garlic, ginger, chilli and sesame oil, and cook, stirring occasionally, for 5 minutes or until the mince is cooked and golden.

2   Remove the pan from the heat and stir in the tamari and spring onion until well combined.

3   Meanwhile, heat the rice according to the packet instructions.

4   Divide the rice, lettuce leaves and beef mixture among serving plates and serve.

CALORIE BOOST PER SERVE

50 calories	1 tablespoon sesame seeds
100 calories	1 carrot + 1 zucchini + ½ small red capsicum
150 calories	180 g cooked sweet potato
200 calories	100 g hokkien noodles

TOTAL 1662 CALORIES   CALORIES 416 PER SERVE

BUDGET BUSTERS

These delicious meals all come in at less than $4 a serve!
How? By featuring loads of fresh seasonal produce and pantry
staples, and using meat sparingly.

BAKED MEATBALLS

PREP 20 MINUTES | COOK 42 MINUTES

This recipe tastes even more delicious if made a day ahead of serving. Cover and
chill overnight, and reheat in a 200°C (180°C fan-forced) oven for 20 minutes.

extra-light olive oil cooking spray
1 carrot, finely chopped
1 zucchini, finely chopped
1 onion, finely chopped
500 g beef mince
1 garlic clove, crushed
1 teaspoon dried mixed herbs
1 × 700 g jar passata
⅓ cup oregano leaves
75 g Danish feta, crumbled
2 cups mixed salad leaves

1   Preheat the oven to 200°C (180°C fan-forced).

2   Spray a deep ovenproof frying pan with oil and heat over high
    heat. Add the carrot, zucchini and onion and cook, stirring
    occasionally, for 10 minutes or until very soft.

3   Meanwhile, using clean hands, combine the mince, garlic and
    dried mixed herbs in a bowl. Season to taste. Roll the beef
    mixture into 12 balls.

4   Add the passata and 1 cup of water to the vegetables in the
    pan. Cook, stirring, for 2 minutes or until the mixture is hot
    and bubbling.

5   Transfer the passata mixture to a 24 cm x 20 cm x 4 cm deep
    baking dish and add the meatballs. Bake for 30 minutes or
    until the meatballs are cooked and golden.

6   Sprinkle the meatball mixture with the oregano and scatter
    with the feta. Serve with salad leaves.

CALORIE BOOST PER SERVE

50 calories	1 tablespoon finely grated mozzarella cheese
100 calories	25 g tasty cheese, grated
150 calories	¾ cup cooked macaroni
200 calories	1½ slices garlic bread

LOW CARB
RECIPE
(less than 14 g per serve)

TOTAL
1490
CALORIES

CALORIES
373
PER SERVE

MUSHROOM AND TOFU SAN CHOY BAO

PREP 15 MINUTES | COOK 10 MINUTES

If time permits, you can marinate the mushrooms, spring onion, ginger and garlic together. Store in an airtight container in the fridge from 20 minutes up to 2 days.

2 teaspoons sesame oil

1 tablespoon peanut oil

500 g sweet potato, cut into 1 cm pieces

400 g firm tofu, chopped

700 g mixed mushrooms, sliced

2 spring onions, thinly sliced

2 cm piece of ginger, finely grated

1 garlic clove, crushed

50 g green beans, thinly sliced crossways

2 tablespoons water chestnuts, finely chopped

⅓ cup oyster sauce

12 iceberg lettuce leaves

1 Heat the sesame and peanut oils in a large non-stick wok. Add the sweet potato and tofu and stir-fry for 5 minutes or until the potato is almost tender.

2 Add the mushrooms, spring onion, ginger and garlic, and stir-fry for 2 minutes. Add the beans, water chestnuts, oyster sauce and ¼ cup of water, and stir-fry for a further 2 minutes or until the vegetables are tender and the sauce reduces slightly.

3 Divide the lettuce leaves among four plates and fill with the mushroom mixture. Serve hot.

CALORIE BOOST PER SERVE

50 calories	1 tablespoon sesame seeds
100 calories	extra 100 g firm tofu
150 calories	⅔ cup cooked egg noodles
200 calories	1¼ cups cooked brown basmati rice

TOTAL CALORIES 1360

CALORIES PER SERVE 340

CHICKEN, PEA AND ZUCCHINI BAKE

PREP 15 MINUTES | COOK 1 HOUR + 5 MINUTES RESTING

If you have leftovers after making this dish, store them in the fridge overnight
and reheat them in the oven or microwave for lunch the next day.

1 cup brown basmati rice

extra-light olive oil cooking spray

100 g white skinless BBQ chicken meat,
finely chopped

1 cup frozen baby peas

1 zucchini, coarsely grated

4 eggs

1½ teaspoons dried mixed herbs

100 g mozzarella, finely grated

2 cups mixed salad greens

1   Place the rice and 2 cups of water in a saucepan and bring to the boil. Reduce the heat and simmer for 15–20 minutes or until the rice is just cooked. Drain, then refresh under cold running water and drain well again.

2   Preheat the oven to 200°C (180°C fan-forced). Spray a 30 cm × 20 cm × 7 cm deep baking dish lightly with oil.

3   Mix the rice, chicken, peas, zucchini, eggs, dried mixed herbs and half the mozzarella together in a large bowl. Season to taste.

4   Transfer the rice mixture to the prepared dish, pressing down firmly. Sprinkle with the remaining mozzarella. Bake in the oven for 40 minutes or until cooked through and golden. Rest for 5 minutes in the dish, then slice and serve warm with salad greens.

CALORIE BOOST PER SERVE

50 calories	1 tablespoon slivered almonds
100 calories	25 g tasty cheese, grated
150 calories	100 g avocado
200 calories	1½ slices garlic bread

TOTAL 1547 CALORIES | CALORIES 387 PER SERVE

CHORIZO-STUFFED SWEET POTATOES

PREP 10 MINUTES | COOK 45 MINUTES

You can swap the sweet potato for a brushed potato, if you like, although
you won't get the added vitamin A boost of sweet potato.

4 × 250 g sweet potatoes, skin on, scrubbed

100 g cured chorizo, finely chopped

1 bunch silverbeet, stems removed
and leaves thinly shredded

1 corn cob, kernels removed

25 g tasty cheese, finely grated

1   Preheat the oven to 200°C (180°C fan-forced).

2   Place the sweet potatoes directly onto an oven rack. Bake for
45 minutes or until tender when tested with a skewer in the
centre. Transfer to serving plates. Split in half lengthways
without cutting all the way through.

3   Meanwhile, place the chorizo in a large non-stick frying pan over
low–medium heat. Cook, stirring occasionally, for 12 minutes
or until the oil slowly releases and the chorizo turns golden.
Add the silverbeet and cook, stirring, for 3 minutes or until the
silverbeet wilts. Add the corn and stir until well combined, then
remove the pan from the heat. Stand, covered, for 2 minutes.
Season to taste.

4   Sprinkle the potatoes evenly with the cheese, then fill with the
chorizo mixture. Serve.

CALORIE BOOST PER SERVE

50 calories	1 tablespoon toasted slivered almonds
100 calories	½ cup full-cream unsweetened Greek yoghurt
150 calories	1 slice garlic bread
200 calories	2 thin slices sourdough

TOTAL 1350 CALORIES

CALORIES 338 PER SERVE

CHICKEN SAUSAGE AND CHICKPEA HOTPOT

PREP 10 MINUTES | COOK 18 MINUTES

This recipe tastes even better when made a day ahead of serving.
Store in an airtight container in the fridge and reheat in a saucepan
over medium heat, adding a little water to loosen if necessary.

500 g chicken sausages

1 × 400 g tin chickpeas, drained and rinsed

2 chicken stock cubes, crumbled

200 g baby red potatoes, thinly sliced

1 zucchini, sliced

1 small red capsicum, seeded
and thinly sliced

½ cup flat-leaf parsley leaves

1   Heat a non-stick saucepan over medium–high heat. Add the sausages and cook, turning occasionally, for 5 minutes or until golden on all sides.

2   Add the chickpeas, stock cubes, potato and 1 litre of water to the pan. Cook, covered and stirring occasionally, for 10 minutes. Add the zucchini and capsicum, and cook, covered and stirring occasionally, for 3 minutes or until just tender. Season to taste.

3   Remove the pan from the heat and stir through the parsley. Serve.

CALORIE BOOST PER SERVE

50 calories	3 teaspoons pine nuts
100 calories	⅔ cup cooked couscous
150 calories	180 g cooked sweet potato
200 calories	1½ slices garlic bread

TOTAL 1466 CALORIES

CALORIES 367 PER SERVE

BUTTER BEAN AND SALMON STEW

PREP 10 MINUTES | COOK 17 MINUTES

You can swap the salmon for skinless chicken thigh fillets or firm tofu.

1 onion, chopped

1 bulb baby fennel, trimmed and sliced

2 garlic cloves, crushed

2 × 400 g tins butter beans, drained and rinsed

2 chicken stock cubes, crumbled

100 g skinless boneless salmon fillet, chopped

1 bunch asparagus, trimmed and cut into 3 cm lengths

1 cup flat-leaf parsley leaves

1   Place the onion, fennel, garlic, butter beans, stock cubes and 1 litre of water in a saucepan over medium heat. Cook, stirring occasionally, for 10 minutes or until the vegetables start to soften.

2   Add the salmon to the pan and stir gently. Cook, covered, for 5 minutes, then add the asparagus and parsley. Stir gently and cook, covered, for a further 2 minutes. Remove the pan from the heat. Season to taste and serve.

CALORIE BOOST PER SERVE

50 calories	1 carrot + ¼ cup baby peas
100 calories	25 g goat's cheese
150 calories	1 cooked potato, chopped
200 calories	1½ slices garlic bread

TOTAL CALORIES 1091 | CALORIES PER SERVE 273

179

CHICKEN PRIMAVERA MACARONI

PREP 15 MINUTES | COOK 10 MINUTES

You can prepare this recipe in full, then transfer to a baking dish and leave to cool before covering tightly and freezing for up to 3 months. Defrost in the fridge overnight before reheating in a 200°C (180°C fan-forced) oven for 20 minutes.

250 g chicken mince

1 zucchini, coarsely grated

2 spring onions, chopped

2 garlic cloves, crushed

200 g sweet cherry tomatoes, thickly sliced into rounds

⅓ cup light pure cream

55 g extra-light spreadable cream cheese

250 g dried elbow macaroni

2 carrots, chopped

300 g broccoli, florets removed and stem chopped

2 cups mixed salad greens

1 Place a large non-stick frying pan over medium–high heat. Add the chicken and cook for 5 minutes, using the back of a spoon to break up any large lumps. Add the zucchini, spring onion and garlic, and cook, stirring occasionally, for a further 5 minutes or until the chicken and vegetables are cooked and light golden.

2 Remove the pan from the heat and stir in the tomato, cream and cream cheese until well combined and the cheese has melted.

3 Meanwhile, cook the macaroni in boiling water for 6 minutes. Add the carrot and boil for 1 minute. Add the broccoli florets and stems and boil for 30 seconds. Drain the macaroni and vegetables, reserving ½ cup of the cooking water. Return the macaroni and vegetables to the pan, keeping it off the heat.

4 Add the hot chicken mixture to the pan and stir until well combined, adding enough of the reserved cooking water to loosen if required. Season to taste. Serve with salad greens.

CALORIE BOOST PER SERVE

50 calories	1 tablespoon finely grated mozzarella
100 calories	2 tablespoons slivered almonds
150 calories	100 g avocado
200 calories	2 thin slices sourdough

TOTAL CALORIES 1697 | CALORIES PER SERVE 424

CHICKEN AND VEGGIE CHOW MEIN

PREP 15 MINUTES + 10 MINUTES STANDING | COOK 10 MINUTES

This is another great idea for lunchboxes. Transport in an airtight container and
keep chilled. Reheat in a microwave on medium heat for 2–3 minutes.

2 carrots

2 zucchini

1 × 375 g packet Singapore-style noodles

225 g chicken breast fillet, diced into
    small pieces

¼ cup oyster sauce

1 tablespoon tomato ketchup

2 garlic cloves, crushed

1 small red capsicum, seeded
    and thinly sliced

2 cups bean sprouts

2 spring onions, thinly sliced

1   Using a julienne vegetable peeler or a spiraliser, cut the carrot
    and zucchini into long thin noodles. Place in a large serving bowl.
    Set aside.

2   Place the noodles in a bowl of boiling water for 10 minutes or
    until they easily separate. Drain, then use scissors to snip into
    5 cm lengths.

3   Place a large non-stick frying pan over high heat. Add the
    chicken and cook for 5 minutes. Reduce the heat to low and add
    the oyster sauce, tomato ketchup, garlic and ¾ cup of water.
    Cook, stirring occasionally, for a further 5 minutes or until the
    chicken is cooked and the sauce slightly reduced.

4   Add the noodles and capsicum to the pan, remove from the heat
    and toss gently to combine.

5   Transfer the noodle mixture to the bowl of carrot and zucchini.
    Add the bean sprouts and spring onion, and toss gently to
    combine. Serve.

CALORIE BOOST PER SERVE

50 calories	1 tablespoon roasted peanuts
100 calories	50 g Malaysian marinated tofu
150 calories	¼ cup raw unsalted cashews
200 calories	200 g cooked peeled prawns

TOTAL CALORIES 1190

CALORIES PER SERVE 298

COCONUT AND ALMOND MACAROONS

PREP 15 MINUTES | COOK 20 MINUTES + COOLING

You can also place the egg-white mixture into a piping bag and pipe rounds
onto prepared trays before baking if you like. It is important to transfer the hot
macaroons from the hot trays to wire racks, otherwise they will stick on cooling.

1 cup desiccated coconut

3 egg whites

½ cup caster sugar

1 teaspoon pure vanilla extract

½ cup almond meal

1 tablespoon self-raising flour

½ teaspoon baking powder

1 Preheat the oven to 180°C (160°C fan-forced). Line two large
   baking trays with baking paper.

2 Remove 2 teaspoons of the coconut and set aside for serving.

3 Place the egg whites in a large bowl and beat with electric
   beaters until soft peaks form. Add the sugar and beat until stiff,
   glossy peaks form. Add the vanilla and beat until just combined.

4 Add the almond meal, coconut, flour and baking powder and
   fold together until well combined. Place dessertspoons of the
   mixture onto the prepared trays, 3 cm apart.

5 Bake for 15–20 minutes until light golden, swapping the trays
   halfway through cooking. Immediately transfer the macaroons
   from the baking trays onto wire racks to cool. Serve, sprinkled
   with reserved coconut.

LOW CARB
RECIPE
(less than 14 g per serve)

TOTAL 1360 CALORIES

CALORIES PER MACAROON 76

EARL GREY GRANITA

PREP 5 MINUTES + COOLING | FREEZE 6 HOURS

The granita will keep stored in the freezer in an airtight container for up to 6 months.

4 Earl Grey teabags
2 tablespoons pure maple syrup
1 cinnamon stick, broken in half
1 litre boiling water
250 g strawberries, hulled and halved
4 ginger snap cookies

1 Place the teabags, maple syrup, cinnamon and boiling water together in a large heatproof jug and stir to combine. Leave until the mixture reaches room temperature.

2 Strain the tea mixture into a glass dish, discarding the teabags and cinnamon. Freeze for 6 hours or until frozen.

3 Using a fork, scrape along the top of the frozen surface to shave the ice. Divide among serving glasses. Serve with the strawberries and ginger snap cookies.

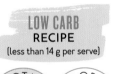

LOW CARB
RECIPE
(less than 14 g per serve)

TOTAL
292
CALORIES

CALORIES
73
PER SERVE

SPRING & SUMMER RECIPES

In the warmer months you want simple, fresh salads and the tangy flavours of ripe seasonal fruit and vegetables. All of these recipes are quick to prepare and cook, so that you don't have to waste a minute that you could be enjoying outdoors in the sunshine.

SMOOTHIE BOWL

PREP 10 MINUTES

This is a great recipe to get children involved with, as they can decorate the top of their own smoothie bowl however they like.

2 frozen large overripe bananas,
   plus 1 fresh banana, sliced lengthways
250 g raspberries
2 tablespoons chia seeds
½ cup chilled coconut water
¼ cup flaked coconut, toasted
¼ cup tiny mint leaves
2 tablespoons flaked almonds

1 Blend the frozen bananas, half the raspberries, the chia seeds and coconut water until thick and smooth. Pour evenly into serving bowls.

2 Top each bowl with the toasted coconut, mint, almonds, extra sliced banana and remaining raspberries. Serve immediately.

CALORIE BOOST PER SERVE

50 calories	2 tablespoons pumpkin seeds
100 calories	1 extra banana
150 calories	½ cup quick oats
200 calories	2 tablespoons 100 per cent almond spread

TOTAL 804 CALORIES   CALORIES 201 PER SERVE

SALMON-WRAPPED ASPARAGUS WITH AVOCADO TOASTS

PREP 15 MINUTES

You can chargrill the asparagus if you like. Simply chargrill over high heat
for 1 minute, turning occasionally, until just tender and bright green.

3 bunches asparagus, trimmed

200 g sliced smoked salmon,
   halved lengthways

8 slices rye sourdough, toasted

2 avocados, sliced

2 teaspoons caraway seeds

2 tablespoons dill leaves

1 lemon, cut into wedges

1 Place the asparagus in a flat heatproof dish. Cover with boiling water and leave for 2 minutes. Drain, then refresh under cold running water. Pat dry with paper towel.

2 Wrap the salmon around the asparagus spears. Season with freshly ground black pepper. Divide among serving plates.

3 Top the toast with avocado and sprinkle with caraway seeds and dill. Season to taste and cut in half.

4 Serve the avocado toast with the salmon-wrapped asparagus and the lemon wedges.

CALORIE BOOST PER SERVE

50 calories	1 tablespoon sour cream
100 calories	3 teaspoons avocado oil
150 calories	2 extra slices rye sourdough, toasted
200 calories	200 g cooked peeled prawns

TOTAL CALORIES 1655

CALORIES PER SERVE 414

LUNCH | SERVES 4

NOODLE SALAD WITH PRAWNS

PREP 15 MINUTES + 5 MINUTES STANDING | COOK 4 MINUTES

For a veggie option, swap the prawns for chopped firm tofu.

2 × 100 g packets dried green
   bean vermicelli noodles

500 g peeled and deveined
   green (raw) king prawns

½ teaspoon sesame oil

2 Lebanese cucumbers, very thinly sliced

2 celery stalks, very thinly sliced

200 g baby mixed tomatoes, sliced

½ cup mint leaves

1 cup small basil leaves

Dressing

2 tablespoons tamari
   (gluten-free soy sauce)

juice of 1 lime

1 tablespoon honey

¼ teaspoon dried chilli flakes

1 tablespoon boiling water

1   Make the dressing by whisking all the ingredients together in a small heatproof jug until the honey has dissolved. Set aside.

2   Place the noodles in a large heatproof bowl. Cover with boiling water and leave for 5 minutes or until the noodles have softened and are translucent. Drain well. Return to the bowl, add the dressing and toss to coat well. Set aside, tossing occasionally.

3   Heat a large chargrill pan over medium–high heat. Place the prawns and sesame oil in a bowl. Season to taste and toss to coat well. Chargrill for 2 minutes each side or until cooked and golden. Transfer to the bowl with the noodle mixture.

4   Add the cucumber, celery, tomato, mint and basil to the noodle mixture and toss gently to combine. Serve warm.

CALORIE BOOST PER SERVE

50 calories	¼ avocado
100 calories	½ cup shelled edamame
150 calories	¼ cup raw unsalted cashews
200 calories	100 g skinless boneless salmon fillet

TOTAL CALORIES 1340 | CALORIES PER SERVE 335

LEMONGRASS BEEF SALAD

PREP 15 MINUTES | COOK 20 MINUTES

Grill the beef and vegetables for this dish on a barbecue
for the perfect summer meal.

1 cup brown basmati rice

500 g diced lean beef

½ teaspoon caster sugar

2 teaspoons ground white pepper

1 stalk lemongrass, finely chopped

1 cm piece of ginger, finely grated

1 green capsicum, seeded
    and thickly sliced

1 red capsicum, seeded and
    thickly sliced

1 red onion, cut into wedges

1 butter lettuce, leaves separated

1 telegraph cucumber, halved
    lengthways, seeds scraped and
    thinly sliced diagonally

½ cup mint leaves

2 limes, halved crossways

1. Place the rice and 2 cups of water in a saucepan and bring to the boil. Reduce the heat and simmer for 20 minutes or until the rice is just cooked.

2. While the rice is cooking, preheat a large chargrill pan over medium–high heat.

3. Place the beef, sugar, pepper, lemongrass and ginger in a bowl and toss together until coated. Chargrill for 4 minutes, turning occasionally, or until golden on all sides. Transfer to a large heatproof bowl and leave to stand, covered.

4. Chargrill the capsicum and onion, in batches, for 3–4 minutes until just tender and golden. Add to the chargrilled beef along with the rice and toss well to combine. Season with salt.

5. Divide the lettuce leaves, cucumber and mint among serving plates and top with the beef mixture. Serve warm, squeezing the lime halves over.

CALORIE BOOST PER SERVE

50 calories	1 tablespoon sesame seeds
100 calories	2 tablespoons roasted peanuts
150 calories	¼ cup raw unsalted cashews
200 calories	extra 1¼ cups cooked brown basmati rice

TOTAL CALORIES 1681

CALORIES PER SERVE 420

FISH SKEWERS AND FENNEL CITRUS SALAD

PREP 20 MINUTES | COOK 4 MINUTES

If time permits, leave the salad to stand at room temperature for
20–30 minutes to allow the flavours to really develop.

300 g skinless boneless salmon fillets,
    cut into 3 cm pieces
300 g skinless boneless white fish fillets,
    cut into 3 cm pieces
2 teaspoons cumin seeds

Fennel citrus salad

3 bulbs baby fennel, trimmed and
    very thinly sliced
2 ruby grapefruits, peeled and
    very thinly sliced
1 orange, peeled and very thinly sliced
1 cup flat-leaf parsley leaves
2 tablespoons red wine vinegar
1 tablespoon extra virgin olive oil

1   To make the fennel citrus salad, place all the ingredients together in a large bowl and toss well to combine. Season to taste and set aside.

2   Preheat a large chargrill pan over medium heat.

3   Place the fish and cumin seeds in a bowl and season to taste. Toss well to coat.

4   Thread the fish evenly among 8 skewers. Chargrill for 4 minutes, turning occasionally, or until the fish is just cooked and golden.

5   Divide the fennel citrus salad among serving plates and top with the fish skewers. Serve.

CALORIE BOOST PER SERVE

50 calories	200 g cauliflower florets, steamed
100 calories	2 tablespoons slivered almonds
150 calories	100 g avocado
200 calories	extra 100 g skinless boneless salmon fillet

LOW CARB
RECIPE
(less than 14 g per serve)

TOTAL CALORIES 1383

CALORIES PER SERVE 346

SERVES 4 | **DINNER**

CHICKEN RISSOLE PARMIGIANA WITH SLAW

PREP 20 MINUTES | COOK 15 MINUTES

Choose a good-quality bolognese sauce with no added sugar.
You can use beef mince instead of chicken mince if preferred.

extra-light olive oil cooking spray

500 g chicken mince

1 zucchini, coarsely grated

2 spring onions, thinly sliced

½ cup packaged dried herb and
    garlic breadcrumbs

1 × 500 g jar bolognese sauce

½ cup finely grated mozzarella

Slaw

¼ cup light sour cream

2 tablespoons lemon juice

2 carrots, coarsely grated

100 g sugar snap peas, thinly
    sliced lengthways

2 celery stalks, thinly sliced diagonally,
    plus inner leaves, chopped

1 small red capsicum, seeded
    and thinly sliced

1   Preheat the grill to high. Lightly grease a deep baking tray with oil spray (this will prevent the sauce from spilling over).

2   Place the mince, zucchini, spring onion and breadcrumbs in a large bowl and mix together until well combined. Season to taste. Divide mixture into 8 portions then, using slightly damp hands, shape and roll into flat rissoles.

3   Heat a large non-stick frying pan over medium heat. Grease lightly with oil. Cook the rissoles for 10–12 minutes, turning only once, until cooked and golden.

4   Transfer the cooked rissoles to the prepared tray. Spoon the bolognese sauce evenly over the rissoles, then sprinkle with the mozzarella. Cook under the grill for 2 minutes or until the cheese has melted and is light golden.

5   Meanwhile, make the slaw by whisking the sour cream and lemon juice together in a large bowl until well combined. Season to taste. Add the remaining ingredients and toss gently to combine.

6   Serve the hot rissoles with the slaw.

CALORIE BOOST PER SERVE

50 calories	1 chicken tenderloin
100 calories	1 slice sourdough
150 calories	35 g tasty cheese, grated
200 calories	1 cup cooked macaroni

TOTAL CALORIES 1633 | CALORIES PER SERVE 408

CHICKEN AND PINEAPPLE RICE SALAD

PREP 15 MINUTES | COOK 30 MINUTES

Another ideal lunchbox salad. Store in an airtight container and keep chilled.

1 cup brown basmati rice

200 g peeled pineapple, chopped

juice of 1 lemon

2 spring onions, thinly sliced

⅓ cup small mint leaves

½ cup small basil leaves

30 g baby rocket leaves

500 g skinless chicken thigh fillets,
   thinly sliced

1 bunch broccolini, trimmed and
   halved crossways

1 Place the rice and 2 cups of water in a saucepan and bring to the boil. Reduce the heat and simmer for 15–20 minutes or until the rice is just cooked. Drain, then refresh under cold running water and drain well again. Place in a large bowl.

2 Add the pineapple, lemon juice, spring onion, mint, basil and rocket to the rice. Season to taste and toss well to combine. Set aside.

3 Place a large non-stick frying pan over high heat. Add the chicken and cook, turning, for 8–10 minutes or until cooked through and golden. Add to the rice mixture and toss together until well combined.

4 Add the broccolini and ¼ cup of water to the same pan. Cook, tossing, for 2 minutes or until just tender and bright green.

5 Transfer the broccolini to serving plates and top with the chicken mixture. Serve with the rice salad.

CALORIE BOOST PER SERVE

50 calories	1½ teaspoons avocado oil
100 calories	1 thin slice sourdough
150 calories	100 g avocado
200 calories	75 g Danish feta

TOTAL CALORIES 1861

CALORIES PER SERVE 465

DINNER | SERVES 4

COCONUT PRAWNS AND ASIAN GREENS SALAD

PREP 20 MINUTES | COOK 8 MINUTES

You can use any combination of Asian greens for the salad.

2 egg whites
750 g peeled and deveined green
    (raw) medium king prawns
½ cup shredded coconut
extra-light olive oil cooking spray

Asian greens salad

1 bunch Chinese broccoli, cut into
    7 cm lengths
3 bulbs baby choy sum, leaves separated
2 tablespoons tamari (gluten-free
    soy sauce)
1 tablespoon mirin
1 cup bean sprouts
2 spring onions, thinly sliced diagonally
1 cup coriander sprigs

1   Make the Asian greens salad. Place the Chinese broccoli and choy sum in a large heatproof bowl and cover with boiling water. Leave for 30 seconds, then drain. Refresh under cold running water and drain well. Transfer to a large serving platter. Top with all the remaining ingredients and set aside.

2   Whisk the egg white in a bowl until frothy, then add the prawns and coconut. Season to taste and toss well to coat.

3   Heat a large non-stick frying pan over medium–high heat. Spray with oil and add the prawns. Cook, turning occasionally, for 8 minutes or until just cooked and golden.

4   Transfer the prawns to the platter with the salad and serve warm.

CALORIE BOOST PER SERVE

50 calories	1 tablespoon sesame seeds
100 calories	1 carrot + 1 zucchini + ½ small red capsicum
150 calories	180 g cooked sweet potato
200 calories	100 g hokkien noodles

LOW CARB
RECIPE
(less than 14 g per serve)

TOTAL
1237
CALORIES

CALORIES
309
PER SERVE

SWEET

SERVES
4

BERRY MERINGUE MESS

PREP 10 MINUTES

Swap the raspberries for other seasonal summer fruits
such as nectarines, peaches or mangoes.

125 g strawberries, hulled
250 g raspberries
2 teaspoons rosewater
350 g full-cream unsweetened yoghurt
4 (10 g) vanilla meringue kisses,
    roughly broken

1   Place the strawberries, half the raspberries and the rosewater
    in a blender and blend to a smooth puree.

2   Transfer the berry puree to a bowl and add the yoghurt and
    meringues. Gently fold together, but do not mix completely as
    you want a lovely berry swirl through the yoghurt.

3   Spoon onto a large platter and serve scattered with the
    remaining raspberries.

TOTAL
572
CALORIES

CALORIES
143
PER SERVE

SUMMER FRUIT SALAD WITH BANANA NICE CREAM

PREP 20 MINUTES

The banana nice cream won't hold its shape for long, so be sure to serve it quickly once blended. You can save the leftover coconut water for smoothies (see pages 82–83). Cover and keep in the fridge to use within 3 days, or freeze for up to 6 months.

1 young coconut
125 g raspberries
120 g blueberries
1 star fruit, sliced
¼ papaya, peeled and sliced
200 g peeled honeydew melon, sliced
2 frozen bananas
2 tablespoons pistachio kernels, chopped
1 lime, cut into wedges

1   Remove the top from the coconut and strain the coconut water into an airtight container. Use a spoon to scoop out the coconut flesh and transfer it to a bowl.

2   Add the raspberries, blueberries, star fruit, papaya and melon to the coconut flesh and stir gently to combine. Divide among shallow serving bowls.

3   Place the frozen bananas and pistachio kernels in a blender. Blend until smooth and creamy. Scoop immediately onto the fruit salad. Serve with lime wedges.

TOTAL CALORIES 677

CALORIES PER SERVE 169

AUTUMN & WINTER RECIPES

As the weather cools down we turn to food for warmth and comfort, but that doesn't mean that it has to be stodgy. The recipes in this chapter make good use of the stovetop, oven and slow-cooker to produce dishes that will warm the cockles of your heart.

SERVES 4 | BREAKFAST/ BRUNCH

GREEN TOAD IN THE HOLE

PREP 15 MINUTES | COOK 8 MINUTES

If you would like a hard yolk, simply cook the stuffed toasts for a further 2–3 minutes, turning once.

300 g baby spinach leaves

2 tablespoons chopped chives

30 g Danish feta, crumbled

4 × 3 cm thick slices sourdough, lightly toasted

extra-light olive oil cooking spray

4 eggs

1   Heat a large non-stick frying pan over high heat. Add the spinach and 1 tablespoon of water. Cook, tossing, for 2 minutes or until wilted. Transfer to a heatproof bowl and add the chives and feta. Season to taste and stir until well combined. Set aside.

2   Using a small knife or 7 cm round cutter, cut a round out of the centre of each piece of toast. Set the rounds and outer pieces of toast aside.

3   Reheat the same frying pan over medium heat. Spray with oil and place the outer pieces of toast into the pan. Fill each toast hole evenly with the spinach mixture, patting down firmly. Crack an egg over the top of the spinach mixture and season to taste. Cook, untouched, for 6 minutes or until the egg whites have set and the yolk is still runny.

4   Transfer the egg toasts to serving plates and serve with the toast rounds for dipping.

CALORIE BOOST PER SERVE

50 calories	extra 25 g Danish feta
100 calories	100 g shredded ham
150 calories	100 g avocado
200 calories	4 short cut bacon pieces

TOTAL 1125 CALORIES | CALORIES 281 PER SERVE

FRUIT COMPOTE WITH RAISIN TOAST AND RICOTTA

PREP 15 MINUTES | COOK 15 MINUTES

You can make a double batch of this compote and keep it
chilled in an airtight container for up to 3 days.

1 red apple, cut into wedges and cored
1 green apple, cut into wedges and cored
2 pears, cut into wedges and cored
⅓ cup craisins
1 cup pure apple and strawberry juice
1 pinch of saffron threads
3 cloves
8 slices raisin bread, toasted
⅓ cup smooth ricotta

1   Place the apple, pear, craisins, juice, saffron, cloves and 1 cup
    of water in a saucepan over medium heat. Cook, stirring
    occasionally, for 15 minutes or until the fruit is tender but
    not falling apart, and the juice is reduced by half. Divide
    among serving bowls.

2   Spread the raisin toast with ricotta and cut into pieces.
    Serve warm alongside the fruit compote.

CALORIE BOOST PER SERVE

50 calories	extra 2 tablespoons smooth ricotta
100 calories	1 banana
150 calories	1½ tablespoons peanut butter
200 calories	extra 2 slices raisin toast

TOTAL CALORIES 1440   CALORIES PER SERVE 360

BAKED ITALIAN CAULIFLOWER

PREP 15 MINUTES | COOK 35 MINUTES

You can take any leftovers to work with you the next day. Simply
reheat in a microwave on medium heat for 2–3 minutes.

500 g cauliflower florets

1 small eggplant, halved lengthways
and sliced

1 × 400 g tin cannellini beans, drained
and rinsed

1 × 700 g jar passata

1 × 400 g tin chopped tomatoes with
herbs and garlic

1 × 225 g jar marinated antipasto
vegetables, undrained

100 g cherry bocconcini, torn in half

2 ciabatta rolls, split in half

1 large garlic clove, halved lengthways

1 cup small basil leaves

1 Preheat the oven to 200°C (180°C fan-forced).

2 Place the cauliflower florets, eggplant and beans in a medium
baking dish (25 cm × 20 cm × 7 cm). Season to taste and toss well
to combine.

3 Place the passata, tomatoes, antipasto and ½ cup of water in
a large jug. Season to taste and stir until well combined. Pour
over the cauliflower mixture in the dish.

4 Bake for 30 minutes, then remove from the oven and top
with the bocconcini. Bake for a further 5 minutes or until the
vegetables are tender.

5 Meanwhile, toast the ciabatta, then rub the cut side of the garlic
clove over the hot toast.

6 Serve the cauliflower bake scattered with the basil, with the
garlic ciabatta alongside.

CALORIE BOOST PER SERVE

50 calories	1 tablespoon finely grated mozzarella
100 calories	25 g tasty cheese, grated
150 calories	1 extra ciabatta roll
200 calories	extra 100 g bocconcini

TOTAL 1808 CALORIES | CALORIES 452 PER SERVE

ONE-PAN ROAST VEGETABLES WITH SALMON CRUMB

PREP 15 MINUTES | COOK 45 MINUTES

You can bake the vegetables ahead of time, then add the salmon crumb and finish
the cooking just before serving (just add an extra 5 minutes to the cooking time).

2 parsnips, trimmed and
   quartered lengthways
2 beetroots, skins scrubbed,
   cut into thin wedges
300 g Brussels sprouts, halved lengthways
2 tablespoons rosemary leaves
¼ cup balsamic vinegar
1 tablespoon pure maple syrup
1 garlic bulb, outer skins removed
   and halved crossways
extra-light olive oil cooking spray
1 × 415 g tin red salmon, drained
2 tablespoons slivered almonds, chopped
1 lemon, cut into wedges
30 g baby spinach leaves

1   Preheat the oven to 180°C (160°C fan-forced). Line a large baking tray with non-stick baking paper.

2   Spread the parsnip, beetroot, Brussels sprouts and rosemary on the prepared tray. Season to taste and toss to combine. Drizzle with the balsamic vinegar and maple syrup, then add the garlic to the tray, cut-side up. Spray lightly with oil. Cover with a piece of non-stick baking paper, then foil. Bake for 30 minutes.

3   Place the salmon and almonds in a bowl and season to taste. Using a fork, roughly mash together.

4   Remove the vegetables from the oven and scatter the salmon and almond mixture over the top. Spray lightly with oil, then return to the oven and bake, uncovered, for 15 minutes or until the vegetables are tender and golden.

5   Serve with the lemon wedges and spinach leaves.

CALORIE BOOST PER SERVE

50 calories	1 extra tablespoon slivered almonds
100 calories	2 extra parsnips
150 calories	150 g chicken tenderloin
200 calories	1 cup cooked macaroni

TOTAL CALORIES 1245   CALORIES PER SERVE 311

SLOW-COOKER CHICKEN SOUP

PREP 15 MINUTES | COOK 4 HOURS

This meal tastes even more delicious when made up to 2 days
ahead of serving to really allow the flavours to develop.

400 g skinless chicken thigh fillets,
   finely chopped
1 bulb baby fennel, trimmed
   and thinly sliced
1 carrot, halved lengthways
   and thinly sliced
1 (200 g) red-skinned potato, chopped
2 celery stalks, thinly sliced
4 spring onions, cut into 3 cm lengths
2 cups reduced-salt chicken stock
¼ cup tarragon leaves
4 small damper rolls

1   Preheat the slow-cooker to high.

2   Add all the ingredients, except the damper rolls, along with
1 cup of water to the slow-cooker. Stir to combine, then cover.
Cook for 4 hours until the chicken and vegetables are tender.
Season to taste.

3   Serve the chicken soup with the damper rolls.

CALORIE BOOST PER SERVE

50 calories	50 g shredded ham
100 calories	25 g goat's cheese
150 calories	1 extra chopped potato
200 calories	50 g cooked chorizo

TOTAL CALORIES 1498 | CALORIES PER SERVE 375

BEEF AND BARLEY SOUP

PREP 15 MINUTES | COOK 35 MINUTES

You can double or triple the quantities for this recipe to make a big batch for freezing. Simply freeze individual portions in freezer-safe resealable food-storage bags for up to 6 months.

1 onion, thinly sliced

1 carrot, finely chopped

2 celery stalks, finely chopped

200 g swede, peeled and finely chopped

2 garlic cloves, sliced

2 sprigs thyme

1 cup pearl barley

1 litre reduced-salt beef stock

200 g thinly sliced rare roast beef

1 bunch English spinach, leaves picked

1 Heat a large non-stick saucepan over medium–high heat. Add the onion, carrot, celery, swede, garlic and thyme. Cook, stirring occasionally, for 5 minutes or until starting to soften.

2 Reduce the heat to medium–low. Add the pearl barley, stock and 2 cups of water to the pan. Cook, partially covered and stirring occasionally, for 30 minutes or until the pearl barley is tender. Remove the pan from the heat.

3 Add the beef and spinach, and stir until the spinach wilts and the beef is heated through. Season to taste, then serve.

CALORIE BOOST PER SERVE

50 calories	3 teaspoons pine nuts
100 calories	75 g rare roast beef
150 calories	180 g cooked sweet potato
200 calories	2 thin slices sourdough

TOTAL 1345 CALORIES

CALORIES 336 PER SERVE

PANKO FISH FINGERS WITH VEGGIE WEDGES

PREP 20 MINUTES + CHILL 20 MINUTES | COOK 40 MINUTES

You can freeze the crumbed, uncooked fish fingers in
an airtight container for up to 3 months.

400 g skinless boneless flathead fillets

1 egg white

1 garlic clove, crushed

1 tablespoon finely chopped chives

1 cup panko (Japanese) breadcrumbs

500 g sweet potato, skin on, scrubbed
    and cut into 1 cm thick wedges

1 large red onion, cut into thick wedges

2 carrots, peeled, quartered lengthways

300 g zucchini, cut into 3 cm pieces

2 teaspoons 'season all' spice mix

extra-light olive oil cooking spray

2 cups baby rocket leaves, to serve

Dipping sauce (Makes ⅔ cup)

⅓ cup light sour cream

1 tablespoon sweet chilli sauce

1 tablespoon tomato ketchup

2 tablespoons lemon juice

1 tablespoon finely chopped chives

CALORIE BOOST PER SERVE

50 calories	1 tablespoon sesame seeds
100 calories	120 g cooked sweet potato
150 calories	⅔ cup cooked egg noodles
200 calories	1¼ cups cooked brown basmati rice

1. Preheat the oven to 200°C (180°C fan-forced). Line two large baking trays with non-stick baking paper.

2. Make the dipping sauce by mixing all the ingredients together until well combined. Chill until required.

3. Cut the fish into 5 cm strips. Whisk the egg white, garlic and chives together in a bowl until frothy, then season to taste. Add the fish strips to the bowl, turning to coat, then add the breadcrumbs. Toss to coat, pressing the breadcrumbs on firmly. Transfer to a plate, cover and chill for at least 20 minutes to set.

4. Meanwhile, place the sweet potato, onion, carrot and zucchini on one of the prepared trays. Spray with oil and sprinkle with the spice mix. Season to taste and toss well to combine, then shake the tray to make sure the vegetables are in a single layer. Bake on the top rack of the oven for 20 minutes, then turn the vegetables over.

5. Transfer the crumbed fish to the remaining prepared tray. Spray lightly with oil. Transfer the tray of vegetables to the bottom rack of the oven and place the fish fingers on the top rack. Bake for 20 minutes, turning the fish once, or until cooked and golden.

6. Serve the fish fingers and veggie wedges with the dipping sauce and baby rocket alongside.

TOTAL 1660 CALORIES   CALORIES 415 PER SERVE

THAI CHICKEN MINI DRUMS AND GREEN RICE

PREP 15 MINUTES | COOK 40 MINUTES + 5 MINUTES STANDING

Mini drumsticks are made from the fleshy part of the chicken wing and take much
less time to cook than legs. Seasoned with herbs and spices, they make tasty
mouthfuls of flavour.

500 g chicken mini drumsticks

1 × 35 g tube fresh Thai herb seasoning

2 carrots, cut into thick matchsticks

1 red capsicum, seeded and
   thickly sliced

extra-light olive oil cooking spray

½ cup reduced-salt chicken stock

Green rice

½ cup brown basmati rice

1 cup reduced-salt chicken stock

1 zucchini, thinly sliced into rounds

300 g broccoli florets

2 spring onions, thinly sliced

1   Preheat the oven to 200°C (180°C fan-forced).

2   Place the chicken, Thai seasoning, carrot and capsicum in
    a baking dish. Season to taste and mix together until evenly
    coated. Spray lightly with oil.

3   Bake for 40 minutes or until cooked and golden. Remove the
    dish from the oven and add the stock. Stir to combine, then rest,
    covered, for 5 minutes.

4   Meanwhile, make the green rice by placing the rice and stock
    in a large saucepan over high heat. Bring to the boil, then
    immediately reduce the heat to the lowest setting possible.
    Cover and cook, untouched, for 15 minutes or until the rice is
    tender. Remove the pan from the heat. Using a fork, fluff and
    separate the grains of rice, then add the zucchini, broccoli and
    spring onion. Stir well to combine. Cover and leave, untouched,
    for 5 minutes. Using a fork, fluff the rice again.

5   Serve the Thai chicken drumsticks with the green rice.

CALORIE BOOST PER SERVE

50 calories	1 tablespoon roasted peanuts
100 calories	2 tablespoons slivered almonds
150 calories	180 g cooked sweet potato
200 calories	100 g hokkien noodles

TOTAL 1512 CALORIES

CALORIES 378 PER SERVE

BAKED CHICKEN PAELLA

PREP 10 MINUTES | COOK 50 MINUTES + 5 MINUTES TO COOL

You can swap the chicken and chicken stock for button mushrooms
and vegetable stock for a vegan-friendly alternative.

extra-light olive oil cooking spray

1 red onion, thinly sliced

1 garlic clove, sliced

1 tablespoon sweet paprika

500 g chicken tenderloins,
    halved crossways

2 cups arborio rice

1 litre reduced-salt chicken stock

½ cup frozen baby peas

⅓ cup flat-leaf parsley leaves

1 lemon, cut into wedges

1 Preheat the oven to 180°C (160°C fan-forced).

2 Heat a 25 cm flameproof and ovenproof baking dish (about 6 cm
deep) with a lid over medium–low heat. Spray with oil. Add the
onion, garlic, paprika and chicken. Cook, stirring occasionally, for
3 minutes or until the onion starts to soften. Add the rice and
cook, stirring, for a further 1 minute. Remove the pan from the
heat. Add the stock and stir well.

3 Transfer to the oven and bake, covered, for 45 minutes or until
the stock has been absorbed and the rice is tender. Remove the
dish from the oven.

4 Scatter the peas over the top and leave, covered, for 5 minutes.

5 Serve the paella scattered with parsley, with the lemon
wedges alongside.

CALORIE BOOST PER SERVE

50 calories	1 carrot + extra ¼ cup baby peas
100 calories	2 (200 g) chicken tenderloins
150 calories	1 slice garlic bread
200 calories	2 thin slices sourdough

TOTAL 1519 CALORIES

CALORIES 380 PER SERVE

SERVES 12

SWEET

RHUBARB CRUMBLE CAKE

PREP 25 MINUTES | COOK 55 MINUTES + COOLING

The cooled cake can be stored in an airtight container, at room temperature, for up to 2 days, or chilled for up to 5 days.

1 bunch rhubarb, trimmed and cut into 5 cm lengths
finely grated zest and juice of 1 orange
½ teaspoon mixed spice
200 g unsalted butter, at room temperature
½ cup caster sugar
2 teaspoons pure vanilla extract
2 eggs, at room temperature
1 cup self-raising flour
¾ cup full-cream milk

Crumble topping

½ cup plain flour
50 g chilled unsalted butter, chopped
¼ cup caster sugar

1   Preheat the oven to 220°C (200°C fan-forced). Line a baking tray with non-stick baking paper. Line the base and sides of a 28 cm × 18 cm slice pan with non-stick baking paper.

2   Place the rhubarb on the prepared baking tray. Sprinkle with the orange zest and juice and the spice. Toss to coat. Bake for 15 minutes or until tender and golden. Leave to cool on the tray. Reduce the oven temperature to 180°C (160°C fan-forced).

3   To make the crumble topping, use your fingertips to rub together the flour and butter to coarse crumbs. Stir through the sugar and chill until required.

4   Beat the butter, sugar and vanilla in a large bowl with electric beaters until pale and creamy. Add the egg and beat until well combined. Add the flour and milk and beat until just combined; do not over mix. Spoon into the prepared slice pan, levelling the surface. Top with the cooled rhubarb mixture and sprinkle with the crumble topping.

5   Bake for 40 minutes or until a skewer inserted into the centre comes out clean. Rest in the pan for 5 minutes, then transfer to a wire rack to cool slightly. Serve warm or at room temperature.

TOTAL CALORIES 3413

CALORIES PER SERVE 284

FUDGY CHOCOLATE AND DATE PUDDINGS

PREP 15 MINUTES | COOK 20 MINUTES + 5 MINUTES TO COOL

You will need 250 g sweet potato for the mash. Peel, then chop into 3 cm pieces
and steam over boiling water for 12–15 minutes until tender, then mash.
You can freeze the cooked, covered puddings for up to 3 months. Defrost in
the fridge overnight, then microwave on medium heat for 2–3 minutes.

extra-light olive oil cooking spray
1 cup mashed sweet potato, cooled
4 Medjool dates, pitted and chopped
⅓ cup cocoa powder
¼ cup rapadura sugar
4 eggs, at room temperature
⅓ cup plain flour
⅓ cup salted caramel ice cream

1   Preheat the oven to 160°C (140°C fan-forced). Spray four ½ cup ovenproof ramekins with oil.

2   Place the sweet potato, dates, cocoa and sugar in a large bowl. Stir together until well combined and smooth.

3   Add the eggs, one at a time, stirring well after each addition until the mixture is well combined. Add the flour and stir until well combined. Spoon evenly among the prepared ramekins, levelling the surfaces.

4   Bake for 20 minutes or until the edges are cooked and the centres are still moist. Cool in the ramekins for 5 minutes, then carefully turn out onto serving plates. Serve warm topped with the ice cream.

TOTAL CALORIES 1249 | CALORIES PER SERVE 312

229

BATCH
IT
UP!

Who doesn't love the idea of saving time? All of these recipes
are designed to be cooked in large batches and frozen in family-meal-
sized portions. They can be reheated and served as is, or transformed
into one of the four suggested variations.

CREAMY CHICKEN AND VEGETABLES

PREP 30 MINUTES | COOK 55 MINUTES

A quarter of this creamy dish serves four people as a meal on its own;
you can freeze the leftovers and use them with one of the creative suggestions
on the following pages.

2 kg chicken thigh fillets, chopped

4 onions, chopped

8 celery stalks, finely chopped

8 zucchini, chopped

8 bulbs baby fennel, trimmed and
thinly sliced

8 garlic cloves, sliced

8 sprigs thyme

4 litres reduced-salt chicken stock

4 × 250 ml tubs '60 per cent
less fat' cream for cooking

400 g baby spinach leaves

1   Heat a large heavy-based stockpot over medium–high heat.
Add the chicken and onion, and cook, stirring occasionally,
for 10 minutes or until the chicken starts to brown and the
onion softens.

2   Add the celery, zucchini, fennel, garlic, thyme, stock and 1 litre
of water. Cook, stirring occasionally, for 45 minutes or until
the chicken and vegetables are very tender and the liquid has
reduced by three quarters. Season to taste.

3   Add the cream and spinach, and stir until well combined and
the spinach wilts.

4   Serve one quarter of the creamy chicken and vegetables as a
meal serving four. Leave the rest to cool to room temperature,
divide into three portions (each serving four) and freeze in
separate airtight containers for up to 6 months.

5   Or you can divide the whole lot into four portions and freeze
for later. Thaw portions in the fridge overnight, then reheat in
a saucepan over low heat until hot and serve, or prepare as the
variation recipes overleaf.

CALORIE BOOST PER SERVE

50 calories	1 tablespoon finely grated mozzarella
100 calories	120 g chopped potato
150 calories	1 ciabatta roll
200 calories	1 cup cooked macaroni

LOW CARB
RECIPE
(less than 14 g per serve)

TOTAL **5796** CALORIES

CALORIES **362** PER SERVE

232

USE ONE QUANTITY OF CREAMY CHICKEN AND VEGETABLES (SEE PAGE 232) TO MAKE EACH OF THESE RECIPES.

LOW CARB
RECIPE
(less than 14 g per serve)

TOTAL
2739
CALORIES

CALORIES
685
PER SERVE

VARIATION 1

> SERVES 4

CHICKEN VOL AU VENTS

PREP 5 MINUTES / COOK 10 MINUTES

Preheat the oven to 200°C (180°C fan-forced). Line a large baking tray with non-stick baking paper and place 4 × 37 g medium-sized vol au vent pastry cases on it. Bake for 10 minutes or until heated and crisp. Transfer to serving plates and divide 1 quantity warmed Creamy Chicken and Vegetables between the cases. Serve with 2 cups mixed salad leaves.

VARIATION 2

> SERVES 4

CHICKEN COTTAGE PIE

PREP 15 MINUTES / COOK 20 MINUTES

TOTAL
1324
CALORIES

CALORIES
331
PER SERVE

Peel and chop 500 g brushed potatoes. Cook in boiling water for 15 minutes or until tender. Drain, then return to the pan and mash roughly with a fork. Season to taste. Transfer 1 quantity warmed Creamy Chicken and Vegetables to a 20 cm square baking dish. Top with potato. Spray lightly with extra-light olive oil cooking spray. Cook under a preheated grill set on high for 2–3 minutes until the top is golden. Sprinkle with parsely and serve with 2 cups mixed salad leaves.

VARIATION 3

CHICKEN FETTUCCINE

TOTAL CALORIES **1845**

CALORIES PER SERVE **461**

PREP 10 MINUTES / COOK 12 MINUTES

Cook 100 g dried fettuccine in a saucepan of boiling water for 10 minutes or until just cooked. Add 100 g trimmed and halved green beans and cook for 1 minute, then drain. Return the pasta and beans to the pan. Stir through 1 quantity warmed Creamy Chicken and Vegetables. Stir in 1 cup basil leaves, sprinkle with thyme sprigs, season to taste and serve.

VARIATION 4

CREAMY CHICKEN WITH SPINACH GARLIC CRUMBS

TOTAL CALORIES **1793**

CALORIES PER SERVE **448**

PREP 10 MINUTES / COOK 5 MINUTES

Cook 100 g chopped fresh garlic bread in a non-stick frying pan over medium heat for 3 minutes or until golden and crisp. Stir in 200 g baby spinach leaves. Cook, stirring, until the spinach wilts. Remove the pan from the heat and stir in 1 cup flat-leaf parsley leaves and 1 tablespoon lemon juice. Season to taste. Serve alongside 1 quantity warmed Creamy Chicken and Vegetables.

SLOW-COOKED BEEF AND VEGETABLES

PREP 30 MINUTES | COOK 1 HOUR 15 MINUTES

A quarter of this rich stew serves four people as a meal on its own;
you can freeze the leftovers and use them with one of the creative suggestions
on the following pages.

2 kg diced 'heart smart' beef

extra-light olive oil cooking spray

4 parsnips, trimmed and chopped

8 carrots, chopped

800 g swede, peeled and finely chopped

⅔ cup rosemary leaves

8 garlic cloves, sliced

4 × 400 g tins chopped tomatoes
  with herbs and garlic

4 litres reduced-salt beef stock

800 g broccoli florets

8 spring onions, cut into 3 cm lengths

1 Lightly spray the beef with oil and season to taste. Heat a large heavy-based stockpot over medium–high heat. Add the beef and cook, stirring occasionally, for 10 minutes or until the beef starts to brown.

2 Add the parsnip, carrot, swede, rosemary, garlic, tomatoes and stock. Cover and cook for 1 hour, or until the beef and vegetables are very tender and the liquid has reduced by about three-quarters, stirring occasionally. Season to taste.

3 Add the broccoli florets and spring onion, and cook, stirring occasionally, for 3 minutes or until the broccoli is just tender and bright green.

4 Serve one-quarter of the slow-cooked beef and vegetables as a meal serving four. Leave the rest to cool to room temperature, divide into three portions (each serving four) and freeze in separate airtight containers for up to 6 months.

5 Or you can divide the whole lot into four portions and freeze for later. Thaw portions in the fridge overnight, then reheat in a saucepan over low heat until hot and serve, or prepare as the variation recipes overleaf.

LOW CARB
RECIPE
(less than 14 g per serve)

CALORIE BOOST PER SERVE

50 calories	3 teaspoons pine nuts
100 calories	1 thin slice sourdough
150 calories	100 g avocado
200 calories	1¼ cups cooked brown basmati rice

TOTAL 4802 CALORIES CALORIES 300 PER SERVE

USE ONE QUANTITY OF SLOW-COOKED BEEF AND VEGETABLES (SEE PAGE 236) TO MAKE EACH OF THESE RECIPES.

VARIATION 1

TOTAL **1730** CALORIES

CALORIES PER SERVE **433**

SERVES 4

MOROCCAN BEEF AND COUSCOUS

PREP 10 MINUTES / COOK 20 MINUTES

Place 1 quantity Slow-cooked Beef and Vegetables in a saucepan over medium heat. Add 1 tablespoon Moroccan seasoning and 1 × 400 g tin drained and rinsed chickpeas. Cook, stirring occasionally, for 15 minutes or until heated. Stir in 200 g baby spinach leaves and cook, stirring, until the spinach wilts. Remove the pan from the heat and stir in ½ cup coriander leaves. Season to taste. Serve with 1 cup cooked couscous.

VARIATION 2

TOTAL **2334** CALORIES

CALORIES PER SERVE **389**

SERVES 6

BEEF CASSEROLE WITH CHEESE DUMPLINGS

PREP 20 MINUTES / COOK 20 MINUTES

Rub 1 tablespoon chilled chopped butter into 1 cup self-raising flour until the mixture looks like breadcrumbs. Stir in 20 g grated tasty cheese, 1 tablespoon finely chopped chives, 1 tablespoon finely chopped flat-leaf parsley and ⅓ cup full-cream milk. Season to taste. Using your hands, knead until the mixture comes together adding 1–2 tablespoons of water if required. Shape into 8 equal-sized balls. Heat 1 quantity Slow-cooked Beef and Vegetables in a heavy-based saucepan over low heat. Top with the cheese dumplings in a single layer. Cook, covered, for 15 minutes or until a skewer inserted into a dumpling comes out clean. Split dumplings and serve with 2 cups mixed salad leaves.

SERVES 4

VARIATION 3

BEEF AND VEGGIE LASAGNE

PREP 15 MINUTES / COOK 40 MINUTES

LOW CARB
RECIPE
(less than 14 g per serve)

TOTAL **1727** CALORIES

CALORIES **432** PER SERVE

Preheat the oven to 200°C (180°C fan-forced). Layer 1 quantity Slow-cooked Beef and Vegetables with 3 fresh lasagne sheets in a 25 cm × 18 cm × 7 cm baking dish. Top with 50 g torn cherry bocconcini. Bake, covered, for 30 minutes or until cooked. Remove cover and brown for 10 minutes. Serve with 2 cups mixed salad leaves.

SERVES 4

VARIATION 4

BEEF POT PIES

PREP 10 MINUTES / COOK 20 MINUTES

LOW CARB
RECIPE
(less than 14 g per serve)

TOTAL **1353** CALORIES

CALORIES **338** PER SERVE

Preheat the oven to 220°C (200°C fan-forced). Fill four 2-cup capacity ovenproof serving bowls with 1 quantity warmed Slow-cooked Beef and Vegetables. Cut 1 thawed sheet of 25 per cent reduced-fat puff pastry into quarters. Lay the pastry over the beef filling in the bowls and brush the pastry tops with 1 beaten egg yolk. Season to taste. Bake for 20 minutes or until the pastry is puffed and golden. Serve with 2 cups mixed salad greens.

DOUBLE ROAST CHICKEN

PREP 20 MINUTES | COOK 1 HOUR 20 MINUTES + 10 MINUTES RESTING

Cooking two chickens at once makes enough for four meals for four to six people; after carving half a chicken for one meal, pull all the remaining meat from the bones and freeze with the leftover vegetables to use for the dishes on the following pages.

8 celery stalks, thickly sliced

4 carrots, halved lengthways and thickly sliced diagonally

4 red onions, peeled and cut into thin wedges

2 × 1.6 kg chickens, rinsed and patted dry

2 lemons, halved

50 g butter, at room temperature

½ cup tarragon leaves, chopped

2 cups flat-leaf parsley leaves, chopped

1 tablespoon sweet paprika

1 garlic bulb, outer skins removed and halved crossways

2 cups reduced-salt chicken stock

1   Preheat the oven to 200°C (180°C fan-forced).

2   Place the celery, carrot and onion in a large roasting tin and sit the chickens on top. Squeeze the juice from the lemons evenly over the chickens, then place inside the chicken cavities. Season all over, to taste.

3   Place the butter, tarragon, parsley and paprika in a bowl. Season to taste. Mix well to combine, then divide the mixture in half. Separate the skin from the breast flesh of the chicken. Push half the butter mixture evenly underneath the skin of each chicken, spreading to cover the entire breast flesh area. Add the garlic and stock to the roasting tin.

4   Bake for 1 hour 20 minutes or until cooked (when a skewer inserted into the thigh meat has juices that run clear and golden). Rest in the roasting tin for 10 minutes.

5   Carve half of one chicken and serve as a meal for four people. Leave the rest to cool to room temperature, then pull all the chicken meat from the bones and divide, along with the vegetables in the tray, into three portions and freeze in separate airtight containers for up to 6 months.

6   Or you can divide the whole lot into four portions and freeze for later. Thaw in the fridge overnight, then reheat in a saucepan over low heat until hot and serve, or prepare one of the variations overleaf.

CALORIE BOOST PER SERVE

50 calories	1 carrot + ¼ cup baby peas
100 calories	2 chicken tenderloins
150 calories	180 g roasted sweet potato
200 calories	2 thin slices sourdough

LOW CARB RECIPE
(less than 14 g per serve)

TOTAL CALORIES 6501

CALORIES PER SERVE 406

USE ONE QUANTITY OF DOUBLE ROAST CHICKEN
(SEE PAGE 240) TO MAKE EACH OF THESE RECIPES.

SERVES 6

VARIATION 1

CHICKEN AND TORTELLINI SOUP

PREP 5 MINUTES / COOK 12 MINUTES

LOW CARB RECIPE
(less than 14 g per serve)

TOTAL **2344** CALORIES

391 CALORIES PER SERVE

Place 1 quantity warmed Double Roast Chicken mixture, half a 360 g packet fresh ricotta and roast vegetable tortellini and 2 litres reduced-salt chicken stock in a large saucepan over medium heat. Cook, stirring occasionally, for 10 minutes or until heated and the tortellini is cooked. Stir in 1 cup basil leaves and 100 g baby spinach leaves until the spinach wilts. Season to taste. Serve.

SERVES 4

VARIATION 2

PULLED CHICKEN BURGERS

TOTAL **2460** CALORIES

615 CALORIES PER SERVE

PREP 10 MINUTES / COOK 5 MINUTES

Split and toast 2 damper rolls. Spread the cut side of the rolls evenly with 2 tablespoons barbecue sauce. Top with 1 quantity warmed Double Roast Chicken mixture, then 4 rings drained tinned pineapple and 4 slices tasty cheese. Grill until cheese melts. Top with 50 g baby rocket leaves and 2 tablespoons finely chopped red onion. Serve.

VARIATION 3

CHICKEN, SPINACH AND FETA FILO ROLL

PREP 20 MINUTES / COOK 30 MINUTES

TOTAL 2309 CALORIES

CALORIES 577 PER SERVE

Wilt 100 g baby spinach leaves with 1 tablespoon lemon juice in a non-stick frying pan over high heat for 1–2 minutes. Cool. Spray 6 filo pastry sheets lightly with extra-light olive oil cooking spray, then stack on top of each other. Sprinkle evenly with 2 tablespoons dried breadcrumbs. Spread with 1 quantity Double Roast Chicken mixture, drained of excess oil, leaving a 3 cm border on all sides. Top with cooled spinach mixture, then 50 g crumbled Danish feta. Fold in the ends and roll up tightly from the long side to form a log. Place the log, seam-side down, on a large baking tray lined with baking paper. Spray lightly with oil. Sprinkle with 1 tablespoon sesame seeds. Bake at 200°C (180°C fan-forced) for 25 minutes or until cooked, crisp and golden. Rest for 2 minutes, then thickly slice. Serve with 2 cups mixed salad leaves.

VARIATION 4

CHICKEN TACOS

TOTAL 2467 CALORIES

CALORIES 617 PER SERVE

PREP 10 MINUTES / COOK 8 MINUTES

Heat 12 corn taco shells on a baking tray in a preheated 200°C (180°C fan-forced) oven for 6–8 minutes or until heated and light golden. Fill with 1 quantity warmed Double Roast Chicken mixture, then 2 cups shredded iceberg lettuce, 1 Lebanese cucumber, thickly sliced diagonally, 1 cup mild salsa and ⅓ cup grated mozzarella cheese.

TOMATO BEANS

PREP 30 MINUTES | COOK 30 MINUTES

A quarter of this tasty vegetable dish serves four people as a meal on its own;
you can freeze the leftovers and use them with one of the creative suggestions
on the following pages.

8 × 400 g tins four-bean mix

3 tablespoons smoked paprika

4 × 700 g jars passata

2 tablespoons dried mixed herbs

8 zucchini, chopped

4 green capsicums, seeded
    and chopped

4 red capsicums, seeded and chopped

4 red onions, chopped

8 carrots, chopped

2 litres reduced-salt vegetable stock

4 cups flat-leaf parsley leaves

1   Heat a large, heavy-based stockpot over medium–high heat.
    Add all the ingredients, except for the flat-leaf parsley, and pour
    in 1 cup of water. Cook, covered and stirring occasionally, for
    30 minutes or until the vegetables are very tender and the liquid
    has reduced by three-quarters. Season to taste.

2   Add the parsley and stir until well combined.

3   Serve one-quarter of the tomato beans as a meal serving four.
    Leave the rest to cool to room temperature, divide into three
    portions (each serving four) and freeze in separate airtight
    containers for up to 6 months.

4   Or you can divide the whole lot into four portions and freeze
    for later. Thaw portions in the fridge overnight, then reheat in
    a saucepan over low heat until hot and serve, or prepare as the
    variation recipes overleaf.

CALORIE BOOST PER SERVE

50 calories	1 tablespoon slivered almonds
100 calories	1 thin slice sourdough
150 calories	100 g avocado
200 calories	1¼ cups cooked brown basmati rice

TOTAL CALORIES 4318

CALORIES PER SERVE 270

USE ONE QUANTITY OF TOMATO BEANS (SEE PAGE 244)
TO MAKE EACH OF THESE RECIPES.

VARIATION 1

SERVES 4

BEAN SOUP WITH PESTO

PREP 10 MINUTES / COOK 15 MINUTES

TOTAL **1554** CALORIES

CALORIES **389** PER SERVE

Heat 1 quantity Tomato Beans, 1 litre reduced-salt vegetable stock and 2 cups water in a saucepan over medium heat. Meanwhile, process 1 cup basil leaves, 30 g baby spinach leaves, ¼ cup grated parmesan, 2 tablespoons roasted slivered almonds, juice of 1 lemon and 2 tablespoons extra virgin olive oil together until smooth. Season to taste. Serve the soup topped with the pesto.

VARIATION 2

SERVES 4

CHEESY BEAN SUBS

PREP 5 MINUTES / COOK 3 MINUTES

TOTAL **1739** CALORIES

CALORIES **435** PER SERVE

Split 200 g baguette in half through the centre. Toast, then top with 1 quantity Tomato Beans. Sprinkle with ⅓ cup grated mozzarella. Grill for 2–3 minutes or until cheese has melted. Serve with 2 cups mixed salad greens.

VARIATION 3

BEAN AND EGGPLANT BAKE

PREP 15 MINUTES / COOK 30 MINUTES

TOTAL 1797 CALORIES

CALORIES 449 PER SERVE

SERVES 4

Layer 2 thinly sliced eggplants and 1 quantity Tomato Beans in a 25 cm × 18 cm × 7 cm baking dish. Spread top with ⅔ cup smooth ricotta and sprinkle with 70 g grated tasty cheese. Bake in a preheated 200°C (180°C fan-forced) oven for 30 minutes or until bubbling and golden. Serve with 2 cups mixed salad leaves.

VARIATION 4

BEAN AND SWEET POTATO CHILLI

PREP 10 MINUTES / COOK 22 MINUTES

SERVES 4

Place 1 quantity Tomato Beans, 500 g chopped sweet potato, 1 teaspoon chilli powder and 2 cups reduced-salt vegetable stock in a large saucepan over medium heat. Cook, covered and stirring occasionally, for 20 minutes or until the sweet potato is tender. Stir in 1 cup cooked brown basmati rice until heated. Serve scattered with ½ cup coriander leaves.

TOTAL 1717 CALORIES

CALORIES 429 PER SERVE

THE LEFTOVER FILES

Here's what to do with all those random leftover pieces of fruit, veggies, protein and pantry staples to turn them into delicious dinner options.

SERVES 4

BREAKFAST/ BRUNCH

IF YOU HAVE

1 large overripe banana **+** 4 strawberries

YOU CAN MAKE

BANANA HOTCAKES WITH STRAWBERRY SAUCE

PREP 15 MINUTES | COOK 10 MINUTES

The more overripe your banana the better, as the fruit
becomes even more sweet as it ripens.

2 cups self-raising flour
2 eggs
1 cup full-cream milk
1 large overripe banana, mashed
extra-light olive oil cooking spray
⅓ cup smooth ricotta

Strawberry sauce

250 g strawberries, hulled
1 teaspoon pure vanilla extract
⅓ cup pure apple and strawberry juice

1 Place the flour, eggs, milk, banana and ¾ cup of water together
   in a bowl. Whisk until well combined. If the mixture is a little
   thick, add a little water to loosen it.

2 Heat a large non-stick frying pan over medium–low heat. Spray
   lightly with oil to grease. Spoon ¼ cup measures of the banana
   mixture into the pan. Cook, in batches, for 1–2 minutes each side
   until cooked, puffed and light golden. Transfer to a plate and
   cover loosely to keep warm.

3 To make the strawberry sauce, place half the strawberries and
   the remaining ingredients in a blender and blend until smooth.

4 Serve the warm hotcakes stacked, drizzled with strawberry
   sauce and topped with ricotta and remaining strawberries.

CALORIE BOOST PER SERVE

50 calories	3 teaspoons pure maple syrup
100 calories	½ cup full-cream unsweetened vanilla yoghurt
150 calories	½ cup full-cream unsweetened vanilla yoghurt + 1 tablespoon slivered almonds
200 calories	2 extra bananas

TOTAL 1546 CALORIES

CALORIES 387 PER SERVE

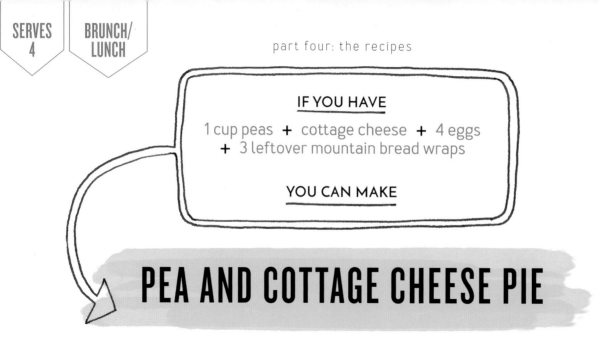

IF YOU HAVE

1 cup peas + cottage cheese + 4 eggs
+ 3 leftover mountain bread wraps

YOU CAN MAKE

PEA AND COTTAGE CHEESE PIE

PREP 15 MINUTES | COOK 30 MINUTES + 5 MINUTES RESTING

You can use ½ teaspoon dried dill instead of fresh dill if preferred.

3 rye mountain bread wraps

4 eggs

1 × 200 g tub cottage cheese

1 cup frozen peas

2 spring onions, thinly sliced

2 tablespoons dill leaves

⅓ cup slivered almonds, toasted

50 g tasty cheese, finely grated

2 cups mixed salad leaves

1   Preheat the oven to 180°C (160°C fan-forced). Line the base and sides of a 20 cm square cake tin with non-stick baking paper.

2   Use 2 mountain bread wraps to line the prepared tin, overlapping in the centre and covering the base and 2 sides of the tin evenly. Cut the remaining wrap in half and use to cover the other two sides of the tin, overlapping with the base.

3   Using a fork, whisk the eggs, cottage cheese, peas, spring onion and dill together in a large jug until well combined. Season to taste, then pour the mixture into the lined pan. Scatter with the almonds, then the tasty cheese. Bake for 30 minutes or until the egg is set at the centre and the mountain bread crust is crisp and light golden. Rest for 5 minutes in the tin.

4   Transfer the pie to a serving plate. Serve warm with the salad leaves.

CALORIE BOOST PER SERVE

50 calories	1 chicken tenderloin
100 calories	1 slice sourdough bread
150 calories	180 g cooked sweet potato
200 calories	100 g skinless boneless salmon fillet

TOTAL 1320 CALORIES

CALORIES 330 PER SERVE

IF YOU HAVE

1 potato + 1 zucchini + 1 carrot + 1 spring onion + fresh herbs + cream

YOU CAN MAKE

CREAMY VEGETABLE SOUP

PREP 10 MINUTES | COOK 18 MINUTES

You can swap the fresh herbs for 1 teaspoon of mixed dried herbs. I use '60 per cent less fat' cream for cooking.

1 (200 g) red-skinned potato, chopped

1 carrot, sliced

1 spring onion, thinly sliced

⅓ cup mixed fresh herbs (parsley, thyme, basil), chopped

2 garlic cloves, crushed

1 litre reduced-salt vegetable stock

1 zucchini, sliced

½ cup '60 per cent less fat' cream for cooking

4 slices garlic bread, toasted

1 Place the potato, carrot, spring onion, herbs, garlic and stock together in a large saucepan over medium–high heat. Cook, partially covered and stirring occasionally, for 15 minutes or until the vegetables are just tender.

2 Add the zucchini and cream. Cook, stirring occasionally, for 3 minutes or until the zucchini is just tender. Season to taste.

3 Serve with toasted garlic bread.

CALORIE BOOST PER SERVE

50 calories	1 tablespoon slivered almonds
100 calories	25 g tasty cheese, grated
150 calories	100 g avocado
200 calories	1½ slices garlic bread

TOTAL CALORIES 1118

CALORIES PER SERVE 280

DINNER | SERVES 4

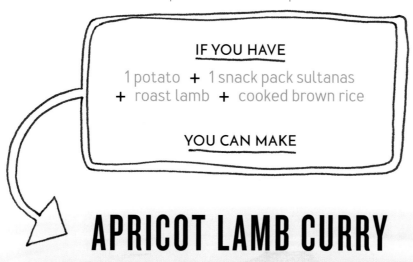

IF YOU HAVE

1 potato **+** 1 snack pack sultanas
+ roast lamb **+** cooked brown rice

YOU CAN MAKE

APRICOT LAMB CURRY

PREP 15 MINUTES | COOK 20 MINUTES

Check the label on the apricot tub – you want pure juice and no added sugar. This meal tastes even more delicious when made up to 2 days ahead of serving to really allow the flavours to develop. Store in an airtight container in the fridge.

300 g leftover roast lamb, chopped
1 (200 g) potato, peeled
  and chopped
1 × 40 g snack pack sultanas
1 tablespoon curry powder
2 × 165 ml tins light coconut milk
½ × 700 g tub apricot halves in juice
100 g baby spinach leaves
1 cup cooked brown basmati rice

1 Place the lamb, potato, sultanas, curry powder, coconut milk, apricot halves and juice in a deep frying pan over medium heat. Cook, covered and stirring occasionally, for 15 minutes or until the potato is tender and the sauce has reduced slightly.

2 Add the spinach. Cook, stirring gently, for 2 minutes or until the spinach wilts. Season to taste.

3 Serve the curry with the rice.

CALORIE BOOST PER SERVE

50 calories	1 carrot + ¼ cup baby peas
100 calories	2 tablespoons toasted slivered almonds
150 calories	extra ½ cup cooked brown basmati rice
200 calories	2 thin slices sourdough

TOTAL 1714 CALORIES | CALORIES 429 PER SERVE

IF YOU HAVE

noodles + 1 tomato + 100 g button mushrooms
+ 2 spring onions + herbs

YOU CAN MAKE

THAI CHICKEN NOODLE SOUP

PREP 10 MINUTES + 5 MINUTES STANDING | COOK 11 MINUTES

If you can't find Thai basil, swap for basil or coriander leaves.

100 g bean thread noodles

100 g rice stick noodles

100 g thin hokkien noodles,
    broken into 3 cm lengths

500 g chicken mince

1 tomato, chopped

100 g button mushrooms

1 litre Thai-flavoured soup base

½ cup basil leaves

1 long red chilli, halved lengthways, seeded
    and thinly sliced (optional)

1   Place the noodles in a large heatproof bowl and cover with
    boiling water. Leave for 5 minutes or until the noodles are
    softened and easily separate. Drain well.

2   Heat a non-stick saucepan over medium–high heat. Add
    the chicken and cook, breaking up any lumps with the back of
    a spoon, for 5 minutes or until cooked through.

3   Add the tomato, mushrooms and soup base to the pan. Cook,
    covered, for 5 minutes, then add the noodles. Cook, stirring,
    for 1 minute or until the noodles are heated through.

4   Serve topped with the basil and chilli, if desired.

CALORIE BOOST PER SERVE

50 calories	1 tablespoon sesame seeds
100 calories	100 g firm tofu
150 calories	⅔ cup cooked egg noodles
200 calories	1¼ cups cooked brown basmati rice

TOTAL CALORIES 1504

CALORIES PER SERVE 376

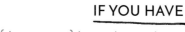

IF YOU HAVE

½ cup panko (Japanese) breadcrumbs + 1 tablespoon basil pesto
+ 1 tablespoon pine nuts + macaroni + broccoli

YOU CAN MAKE

CRUNCHY PESTO WINGS AND BROCCOLI PASTA

PREP 20 MINUTES | COOK 50 MINUTES

You can make this recipe with chicken tenderloins instead of chicken wings if desired.

8 small chicken wings
¼ cup panko (Japanese) breadcrumbs
1 tablespoon basil pesto
1 tablespoon pine nuts, chopped

Broccoli pasta

125 g dried elbow macaroni
400 g broccoli florets
1 cup small basil leaves
juice of ½ lemon
20 g parmesan, finely grated

1 Preheat the oven to 200°C (180°C fan-forced). Line a large baking tray with non-stick baking paper. Place the chicken wings on the prepared tray. Bake for 30 minutes.

2 Place the panko, pesto and pine nuts in a bowl. Season to taste and stir until well combined. Sprinkle over the chicken wings. Bake for a further 20 minutes or until the chicken is cooked and golden.

3 Meanwhile, to make the broccoli pasta, cook the macaroni in a large saucepan of boiling water for 6 minutes. Add the broccoli and cook for a further 2 minutes. Drain well, then return to the pan, off the heat. Add the basil, lemon juice and parmesan. Season to taste and stir until well combined.

4 Divide the broccoli pasta among serving plates and top with the chicken wings. Serve.

CALORIE BOOST PER SERVE

50 calories	1 carrot + ¼ cup baby peas
100 calories	25 g goat's cheese
150 calories	1 slice garlic bread
200 calories	2 thin slices sourdough

TOTAL CALORIES 1275 | CALORIES PER SERVE 319

IF YOU HAVE

2 bacon rashers + ½ cup peas + 1 sweet potato + 50 g Brussels sprouts + beef fillets

YOU CAN MAKE

STEAK WITH BACON AND POTATO HASH

PREP 10 MINUTES | COOK 12 MINUTES + 5 MINUTES RESTING

Choose the barbecue sauce with the lowest sugar content. You can add a red onion to the hash for extra sweetness if you like.

300 g sweet potato, chopped

1 onion, cut into thin wedges

2 rindless bacon rashers, sliced

½ cup frozen baby peas

50 g Brussels sprouts, thinly sliced into rounds

1 tablespoon Worcestershire sauce

2 tablespoons barbecue sauce

4 × 150 g beef fillet steaks, seasoned

1   Heat a large non-stick frying pan over medium–high heat. Add the sweet potato, onion and bacon. Cook, stirring occasionally, for 10 minutes or until cooked and golden. Reduce the heat to low.

2   Add the peas, Brussels sprouts, sauces and ½ cup of water to the pan. Cook, tossing, for 2 minutes. Season to taste.

3   Meanwhile, heat a large chargrill pan over medium–high heat. Chargrill the steaks for 3 minutes on each side for medium. Transfer to serving plates, cover loosely with foil and leave to rest for 5 minutes.

4   Serve the steak with the bacon and potato hash.

CALORIE BOOST PER SERVE

50 calories	1 carrot + ¼ cup baby peas
100 calories	25 g goat's cheese
150 calories	1 chopped cooked potato
200 calories	1 cup cooked macaroni

TOTAL CALORIES 1379

CALORIES PER SERVE 345

IF YOU HAVE

500 g mince **+** ½ cup leftover mashed potato
+ ½ carrot **+** 1 celery stalk

YOU CAN MAKE

EVERYTHING MEATLOAF

PREP 20 MINUTES | COOK 50 MINUTES + 5 MINUTES RESTING

You can swap the beef mince for kangaroo mince, chicken mince, pork and veal
mince or a combination of whatever you have to hand.

500 g beef mince

1 egg

2 tablespoons tomato ketchup,
   plus ⅓ cup extra for serving

½ cup mashed potato

½ carrot, grated

1 celery stalk, finely chopped

150 g peeled pumpkin, grated

300 g broccoli, cut into 1 cm
   thick slices

2 corn cobs, thickly sliced

200 g green beans, trimmed

30 g butter

sprigs of thyme and oregano, to serve

1 Preheat the oven to 200°C (180°C fan-forced). Line the base and sides of a 22 cm × 10 cm × 7 cm loaf tin with non-stick baking paper.

2 Put the mince, egg, ketchup, potato, carrot, celery and pumpkin together in a large bowl. Season to taste and mix until well combined. Press the mixture firmly into the prepared tin.

3 Bake for 45–50 minutes until golden and cooked when tested at the centre with a skewer. Rest in the tin for 5 minutes.

4 Meanwhile, while the meatloaf rests, blanch the broccoli, corn and beans in boiling water for 3 minutes or until just tender. Drain, then place in a heatproof bowl. Add the butter, season to taste and toss to coat well.

5 Serve the sliced meatloaf with the extra ketchup and the vegetables. Scatter with thyme and oregano sprigs.

CALORIE BOOST PER SERVE

50 calories	3 teaspoons pine nuts
100 calories	1 slice sourdough
150 calories	100 g avocado
200 calories	1 cup cooked macaroni

TOTAL 1777 CALORIES | CALORIES 444 PER SERVE

SERVES 4

SWEET

IF YOU HAVE

2 cups cooked brown rice
+ chocolate hazelnut spread + cream

YOU CAN MAKE

CHOC-HAZELNUT CREAMED RICE

PREP 5 MINUTES | COOK 5 MINUTES

This recipe tastes delicious made with leftover cooked jasmine rice or medium-grain white or brown rices: just remember to adjust calorie counts according to the different types of rice. I use '60 per cent less fat' cream for cooking.

2 cups cooked brown basmati rice
¼ cup chocolate hazelnut spread
½ cup '60 per cent less fat'
   cream for cooking
125 g raspberries

1   Place the rice, hazelnut spread and cream in a saucepan over low–medium heat. Cook, stirring, for 5 minutes or until well combined and hot.

2   Serve topped with raspberries.

TOTAL CALORIES 1160

CALORIES PER SERVE 290

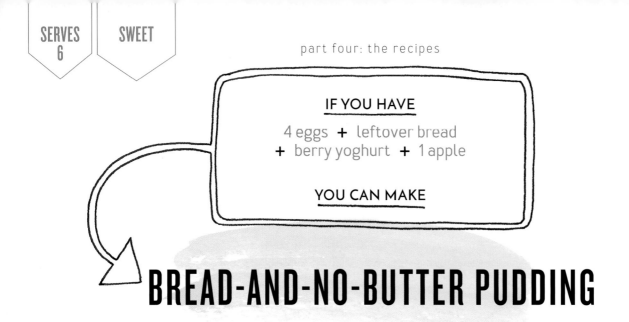

IF YOU HAVE

4 eggs + leftover bread
+ berry yoghurt + 1 apple

YOU CAN MAKE

BREAD-AND-NO-BUTTER PUDDING

PREP 10 MINUTES + 10 MINUTES STANDING | COOK 40 MINUTES + 5 MINUTES RESTING

Use whatever leftover bread you like here: sourdough, raisin
bread or English muffins. Leftover serves are great as a breakfast
treat. The berry yoghurt should contain no added sugar.

extra-light olive oil cooking spray

4 eggs

175 g full-cream unsweetened berry yoghurt

2 cups unsweetened almond milk

2 teaspoons pure vanilla extract

1 red apple, coarsely grated

1 slice sourdough, cut into 3 cm pieces

2 slices raisin bread,
   quartered into triangles

1 English muffin, split and cut into wedges

1 teaspoon pure icing sugar

1   Preheat the oven to 180°C (160°C fan-forced). Spray
    a 25 cm × 15 cm × 7 cm baking dish with oil.

2   Using a fork, whisk the eggs, yoghurt, milk, vanilla and apple
    together in a large bowl until well combined.

3   Add the sourdough, raisin toast and muffin pieces to the egg
    mixture. Toss together to coat well. Transfer the mixture to
    the prepared dish, making sure the bread pieces are separated
    and evenly spaced over the dish. Stand for 10 minutes to allow
    the egg mixture to soak into the bread.

4   Bake for 35–40 minutes or until set and golden. Rest for
    5 minutes in the dish and serve warm dusted lightly with
    the icing sugar.

TOTAL 1115 CALORIES

CALORIES 186 PER SERVE

PART FIVE

THE
WORKOUTS

Unless you've been living under a rock, you'll know there are myriad reasons why exercise is good for you and why it should be a consistent part of your life. I'm not going to hammer on about every single reason here, but instead just recap the major points.

Strength training is critical for bone density, which is a big win in the war against osteoporosis and brittle bones. It also builds muscle mass, and the more of this you have, the higher your metabolic rate will be, which is a win for keeping your body fat down to healthy levels.

Cardio training is how you keep your heart and lungs healthy, which gives you the energy and vitality to tackle your life at full tilt. Exercising with your family is play, so it doesn't feel like a chore and everybody gets the benefits of exercising in a fun and relaxed manner. It also deepens family connections, not to mention reinforcing to the kids that moving is fun, is lifelong and is for everyone!

Trust me, feeling strong and fit in your body is an awesome feeling – you have the power, pep and passion to keep up with your busy life. Who doesn't want to feel like that? Like they're on top and in control, rather than squashed flat and at the mercy of their lives.

I've trained thousands of people over the years, and have spent a lifetime training myself, and I can tell you that consistent exercise (both strength and cardio) is a key component in weight loss and subsequent weight maintenance. Combine it with consistently healthy food choices and you are setting yourself up for success that will last a lifetime!

LISA'S STORY

I have been overweight forever but never considered myself anything more than 'big boned' or just tall with a presence. I am 5'9' (176 cm) and was 102.5 kg when I first weighed myself pre-season. I carried that weight well and had confidence but knew I felt uncomfortable at the beach or exposing my arms or stomach. I live in London, but am from Brisbane, and three friends had lost 10 kg+ on 12WBT and so I thought maybe I should try it. I had tried Weight Watchers, fad diets, counting calories, etc, and they all had some success but then the weight returned, so I thought I would give it a go and see if I could lose some weight. I had never done anything online before so this was new! Why? I just wanted to feel comfortable in my own skin.

I decided my goal weight was going to be 72.5 kg because that would be exactly 30 kg lost. It was in the healthy weight range and seemed a distant dream. I reached that in just over 12 months. I maintained that for 12 months – and it wasn't actually all that hard! I used all the tools I had learnt. I did one round of 12WBT and did the rest on my own using the recipes I had, logging everything into MyFitnessPal, joining Facebook groups like 12WBT Runners Connect and 12WBT 30 Plus Crew. I was inspired by the stories.

I fractured my ankle in October and due to not being able to run, wearing a moonboot, and then Christmas, I managed to put on 5 kg. I ate like I was still running five times a week. I went to a lot of Christmas events, ate high-calorie food and drank more alcohol than usual. Low-impact exercising just doesn't burn the same amount of calories! I tried to make low-impact exciting by mixing it up and doing yoga, swimming, core workouts, low impact HIIT and walking. All that did was make me miss running!

But I was on the case and doing high-impact exercise as soon as my ankle had healed, and with the help of Voome recipes, the weight is coming off again. I know what to do and I love my new lifestyle and healthy way of living. I can't go back!

I couldn't run 1 km before – now I have done six half marathons and have an entry into the New York Marathon!

Mish says...

Lisa's injury set her back but she knows what she needs to do to get back into the groove. She has her environment sorted and her new-found passion for exercise will stand her in good stead.

STRENGTH EXERCISES

All these strength exercises are fundamentals. They get your whole body working as a unit and recruit all your major muscle groups. They improve your strength and posture, and allow you to power through life! You don't need to have a gym membership or fancy equipment – just a simple set of weights will do it. The exercises can be done at home or at a park.

Aim to do strength training two to three times a week

The beauty of the strength exercises featured here is that you can choose how you want to put them together in your workout.

> → You could do, say, an AMRAP (as many rounds as possible) of 10 minutes' duration. So, you would do five reps of each exercise to complete one round, then go back to the start and keep cycling through in the time allowed. Keep count of the number of rounds you get through and try to beat it next time. You might choose to make it ten reps of each exercise if you had time to do a 20-minute AMRAP.

> → You could do a workout of 2 minutes for each exercise (see how many reps you get through of each exercise in 2 minutes) which would give you a 16-minute workout. Or, if you're short on time, just do 1 minute of each and you have an 8-minute workout.

> → If you wanted to do a more 'old school'/traditional-style workout, you could do three sets of eight to ten reps of each exercise. You could choose one of two ways: the first is to do three circuits of each set (so one set of eight to ten reps of squats, then one set of eight to ten reps of deadlifts, and so on, then once you've completed your one set of eight to ten reps of planks, have a break of 1–2 mins, then start your next circuit, then one more circuit and that's your workout done!). Or you could do three sets of squats with a rest of 1 minute in between each set, then move onto the deadlifts and do your three sets of those, and so on.

SQUATS

Stand with your feet shoulder-width apart, knees over toes, chest up, belly braced and eyes on the horizon.

Push your hips back and squat down as far as you can while keeping your knees in line with your toes, your chest up, belly braced and eyes forward (if you lose any of these key posture points, you know you have gone too deep in your squat). Squeeze your butt, press firmly through your feet and return to your start position.

DEADLIFTS

(can be done with either dumbbells or barbells)

Stand with your feet hip-width apart, chest up, belly braced and eyes on the horizon. Hold the weights in your hands just at the outside edges of your thighs.

Hinge from the hips, pushing your butt back and keeping your back flat. As your torso tips forward, keep it braced and let the weights slide down your thighs to your knees. Your gaze should be fixed on the ground in front of you. Squeeze your butt, press firmly through your feet and return to your start position, letting the weights slide back up your thighs.

DEADROWS

(can be done with either dumbbells or barbells)

Stand with your feet hip-width apart, chest up, belly braced and eyes on the horizon. Hold the weights in your hands just at the outside edges of your thighs.

Hinge from the hips, pushing your butt back and keeping your back flat. As your torso tips forward, keep it braced and let the weights slide down your thighs to your knees. Your gaze should be fixed on the ground in front of you.

In this position, squeeze your back and pull your elbows up to row the weights into your hip crease. Stay in this tilted position and slide the weights back down to your knees. Squeeze your butt, press firmly through your feet and return to your start position, letting the weights slide back up your thighs.

TABLE PULLS

Shimmy yourself under a sturdy table, gripping the edges firmly with your hands at shoulder level, with your arms long and your feet placed hip-width apart. For beginners/intermediate level, place your feet on the floor with your knees bent. For intermediate/advanced level, place your feet on the floor with your legs straight.

Keeping your belly braced, pull yourself up until your face is close to the underside of the table, squeezing your back, butt and hamstrings. Lower yourself back down to your start position slowly.

If you're at a park, look for equipment you can use to pull up against, such as a bar. Alternatively, wrap a towel around a tree and do your pull ups that way.

PUSH UPS

Starting on your knees or toes, place your hands on the floor in front of you, slightly further than shoulder-width apart and just behind the top line of your shoulders. Keep your body straight, draw your shoulder blades down away from your ears, brace your belly and look at the floor just in front of your hands.

Lower your chest towards the floor as far as you can – if you lose any of these key posture points, you know you have gone too low, so adjust your position next time.

Push firmly through your hands, squeeze through your chest and come back up to your starting position.

OVERHEAD PRESS

(can be done with either dumbbells or barbells)

Stand with your feet hip-width apart, chest up, belly braced and eyes on the horizon. Hold the weights with your hands at the top of your chest, with your elbows pointing down and tucked in close to your body.

Push the weights up until your arms are fully extended, then lower the weights back down to the start position.

PLANKS

Planks are done as a static hold of 30 seconds for beginners, 1–2 minutes for intermediate and 2 minutes (or more*) for advanced.

*Advanced peeps remember, this is not a competition as to how long you can hold a plank, it's a strength training exercise as part of an overall workout, so you don't want to be holding the plank to failure (unless you have stacks of time – because you might be holding that baby for a loooooong time).

On your knees or toes, place your hands or forearms on the floor in front of you, directly under your shoulders. Draw your shoulder blades down away from your ears, brace your belly, squeeze your butt and look at the floor just in front of your hands.

Hold this position for as long as you can maintain these key posture points.

CARDIO EXERCISES

All these exercises are crackers – they fire your cardiovascular system, improve your fitness and coordination and allow you to energise your life!

Aim to do cardio workouts three to four times a week. If you do three strength sessions a week, then only do three cardio sessions; you need one rest day every seven days. If you do two strength sessions a week, you can do four cardio sessions.

Cardio sessions can be as long as you have time for – what's important (as with the strength sessions) is that you can fit them into your life, so you actually do them!

1 RUNNING

2 CYCLING

3 ROWING

4 SKIPPING

5 BOXING

281

NO-EQUIPMENT WORKOUTS

STRENGTH & CARDIO

LOUNGEROOM WORKOUT

As many sets as possible (in the time you have) of the following five exercises. Your warm up is 2 minutes skipping (without a rope):

1   <u>1 MINUTE SKIPPING</u>

With these and the park workouts, if you only have time to do one round of each, allow 1 minute to complete ten reps then move to the next exercise), so you would be done in 10 minutes, allowing 2 minutes at the end to stretch).

If you have longer, just cycle through the workout in the time you have. So:

→ 2 minutes warm up, 2 minutes stretch at end + 6 minutes of work (one round) would be a 10-minute workout

→ 2 minutes warm up, 2 minutes stretch at end + 12 minutes of work (two rounds) would be an 18-minute workout

→ 2 minutes warm up, 2 minutes stretch at end + 18 minutes (three rounds) would be a 20-minute workout, etc.

easier: fast walk on the spot

harder: double-unders (whipping the skipping rope around twice under your feet when you jump)

2   TEN SQUATS

easier: wall-sit for as long as you can, then rest, and repeat ten times

(how to wall-sit: sit with your back against a wall and slide down until you are in a seated position, with your butt as close to level with your knees as possible. Make sure your ankles are lined up under your knees, your legs are hip-distance apart, and your head is lined up over your shoulders: no forward head tilt!)

harder: hold each squat at the bottom and pulse ten times

3   TEN PUSH-UPS ON YOUR KNEES

easier: against a wall (place your hands shoulder-width apart on the wall, with your feet stepped back from the wall enough that you have room to bend your elbows and take your torso to the wall. Bend your elbows and, keeping your body in one line, bring your torso towards the wall. Then, pressing strongly through your arms and squeezing with your chest, push back to your start position)

harder: on your toes

4   TEN ROLLING BRIDGES WITH A 10-SECOND HOLD AT THE TOP

easier: no hold at the top

harder: single leg, five each side (lift one leg straight up into the air – imagine you're trying to point your toes or flex your foot to touch the sky as you perform the movement, rolling your spine up off the ground from your butt to the back of your shoulders, then rolling back down). Keep your leg in the air for five reps (one rep is rolling up and rolling down), then swap straight over to the other leg and repeat for five reps.

5 TEN TRICEP DIPS

easier: keep your butt on the floor

harder: single leg lifted, alternating

6 TEN WINDSCREEN WIPERS

easier: don't take your knees all the way to the floor

harder: straight legs rather than bent legs

PARK WORKOUT

Warm up: 2 minutes skipping
(without a rope). Then five sets
of the following:

CARDIO & CONDITIONING

1   TEN FROG JUMPS

easier: step, don't
jump

harder: jump higher
and further

2   TEN RUSSIAN TWISTS (L+R = ONE)

easier: single-hand
touches, same hand,
same side

harder: both feet off
the ground

286

3   TEN BEAR CRAWLS

easier: crouch walk

harder: keep lower to the ground

4 TEN ICE SKATERS (L+R = ONE)

easier: step, don't jump

harder: jump higher, land with a deeper leg bend

5 TEN TRICEP DIPS

easier: butt on ground

harder: single leg lifted, alternating

6   TEN HAND-RELEASE PUSH-UPS

easier: on your knees

harder: push up and clap

289

KIDS' GAMES WORKOUT

Play as many of these as you and the kids have the energy and time for!

1 DROP AND GIVE ME TWENTY

Everyone runs, hops or skips until the whistle blows, then you do twenty of either:

- → Touch the ground, touch the sky

- → Rainbows (aka touchdowns)

- → Walk outs, walk ins

Repeat until everyone has had a go being the whistleblower and has done one each of all the options.

2 TAG

You'll need a group of at least three people. One person is 'it', and they run around trying to catch, or tag, the others. When they succeed, that person becomes 'it' and the game continues.

3 LEAP FROG

Line up and, on the whistle, the first person runs forward and bobs down. On the next whistle the next person in line runs forward and leap-frogs over the crouched person (who then runs to the back of the line). The whistle blows again and the next person runs forward and leaps over the crouched person (who then runs to the back of the line). Take turns until everyone has had a go at being the whistleblower, has been leapfrogged over and has been the frog!

4 TUNNELLING

Everyone kneels (the smaller kids can stand) in two lines facing each other and holding hands with the person opposite. The pair at one end of the line have to crawl through the tunnel formed by everyone else, then pop out at the other end and line up again to form the tunnel. Play until everyone has been through the tunnel.

5 CHAIR CIRCLES

Have everyone form a circle and dance around in a clockwise direction until the whistle blows. At the whistle, everyone faces the back of the person in front of them (like dominoes) and then everyone carefully sits down on the knees of the person behind them. Hold until the chairs fall over! Whistle blows again when the chairs collapse and everyone dances around in a clockwise direction until the whistle blows again. This time everyone faces outwards, links elbows and sits down as though on a chair. Hold until the chairs fall over!

6 ELASTICS

Just like we used to do in the playground. England-Ireland-Scotland-Wales, inside-outside-monkey's-tails! 2 minutes jumping time per person.

7 SKIPPING

Again, just like we used to do in the playground with a single big rope (or go for gold and have doubles!). The skipper can skip for as long as they can or 2 minutes (whichever is the lesser). Repeat until everyone has had a go.

Take every opportunity you can to MOVE! It's what your body is designed to do. Slot one or two of these incidental activities in *every day*.

→ walk to work (think of the money you'll save)

→ walk to a bus stop one or two stops further away than your usual stop

→ take the stairs instead of the escalator or elevator

→ hang the washing out and bring it in

→ do wall-sits (see page 283) while you brush your teeth

→ lunge up and down the hallway instead of walking

→ do squats while you wait for the kettle to boil/pasta water to boil/microwave to do its thing

ACKNOWLEDGEMENTS

I would like to thank the following who have helped make this book a reality:

Gabi Bruce from Team MB, and Jane Weston and Joseph Hanrahan from Chic Talent Management.

The team at Pan Macmillan: Ingrid Ohlsson, Virginia Birch, Megan Pigott, Naomi Van Groll, Ariane Durkin and Sally Devenish.

Recipe developer Tracey Pattison, editor/writer Miriam Cannell, designer Emily O'Neill, photographer Rob Palmer, assistant photographer Mal Lyons, stylist David Morgan, Simone Forte Hair and Make Up, CM Stylists and nutritionist Marieke Rodenstein.

Professor Katherine Samaras for her time and generosity.

My 12WBT Team, its amazing members and my incredibly giving clients who shared their stories.

My patient and loving family, and those who have been supporters of my programs and books over the years.

INDEX

First published 2017 in Macmillan
by Pan Macmillan Australia Pty Limited
1 Market Street, Sydney, New South Wales
Australia 2000

A CIP catalogue record for this book is available from the
National Library of Australia: http://catalogue.nla.gov.au

Design by Emily O'Neill
Photography by Rob Palmer
Prop and food styling by David Morgan
Recipe development by Tracey Pattison
Nutritional analysis by Marieke Rodenstein
Editing by Miriam Cannell and Ariane Durkin
Fashion styling by CM Stylists
Makeup by Simone Forte
Colour + reproduction by Splitting Image Colour Studio
Printed in China by Imago Printing International Limited

10 9 8 7 6 5 4 3 2 1

We advise that the information contained
in this book does not negate personal
responsibility on the part of the reader
for their own health and safety. It is
recommended that individually tailored
advice is sought from your healthcare
or medical professional. The publishers
and their respective employees, agents
and authors are not liable for injuries
or damage occasioned to any person
as a result of reading or following the
information contained in this book.

MICHELLE'S STORY

In her nearly 30 years in the health and fitness industry, Michelle Bridges has focused on breaking down the barriers that block the path to a happier and healthier life. Her 12 Week Body Transformation is Australia's most successful online weight-loss program, and has helped Australians lose more than 1.5 million kilos. She is the bestselling author of 13 books on nutrition and fitness, including *Food for Life*.